SACRAMENTO PUBLIC LIBRARY

3 3029 00551 5812

CEN 951.9 W424 1976
1
Weintraub, War in the wards :
2d ed. Presidio Press, c1976.
3 3029 00551 5812

951.9
W424
1976   Weintraub   895
          War in the wards
                               c.1

CENTRAL
JAN 2 5 1978

SACRAMENTO PUBLIC LIBRARY
SACRAMENTO, CALIFORNIA

WAR IN THE WARDS

Other works by Stanley Weintraub include:

Private Shaw and Public Shaw: A Dual Portrait of Lawrence of Arabia and G.B.S.

Aubrey Beardsley: Imp of the Perverse

The Last Great Cause: The Intellectuals and the Spanish Civil War

Evolution of a Revolt: Early Postwar Writings of T. E. Lawrence (ed. with Rodelle Weintraub)

Shaw: An Autobiography 1856-1898 (ed.)

Whistler. A Biography

Lawrence of Arabia: the literary impulse (ed. with Rodelle Weintraub)

Journey to Heartbreak. Bernard Shaw 1914-1918

Four Rossettis. A Victorian Biography

WAR IN
THE WARDS

*Korea's Unknown Battle in a
Prisoner-of-War Hospital Camp*

STANLEY WEINTRAUB

PRESIDIO PRESS
San Rafael, California

Library of Congress Catalog Card Number 76-51509
ISBN 0-89141-012-0
Copyright © 1976

PRESIDIO PRESS
1114 Irwin Street, San Rafael, CA

All Rights Reserved
Printed in the United States of America
Second Edition

Sketches by Stephen A. Farris

CENTRAL

with gratitude and affection,
to those servicemen—regular and reluctant—
whose personalities and activities,
but not whose names,
make up the Korean chronicle
which is this book

"... *it had a strange, exciting*
quality, rather like that of a
clear dream."

—from my Korean notes, quoted
from an otherwise irrelevant short
story by J. B. Priestley, "The
Curtain Rises," in a much-worn issue
of *Collier's* (Oct. 27, 1951).

Contents

List of Illustrations

WAR IN THE WARDS

Foreword

Toward the close of 1952, *Pravda* reported once more the savage American treatment of Communist prisoners of war in Korea. The news intrigued those of us in the Prisoner-of-War Command both because of its absurdity and its paradoxical reflection of our frustration-born wishful thinking. One charge asserted that 1,400 prisoners of war had been secretly sent to the United States "for atomic weapons to be tried out on them." Another specified that "in May this year new types of flame throwers were tried out on prisoners of war" and that 800 prisoners had paid for their expressed desire for repatriation by being burned alive. The foreign news page of *Pravda* featured a cartoon titled "American benevolence" portraying a bleeding, half-naked Korean war prisoner lashed to a post. In front of him stood a two-star American general armed with a gore-splashed revolver, a monstrous hypodermic, bloody handcuffs and thick whip. The general held up the prisoner's bloody hand and said, "Look, he doesn't want to be repatriated." Another Soviet cartoon depicted a gangster-like, helmeted GI with submachine gun, leading a group of burly soldiers over the bodies of prisoners to hold back others with their rifle butts. The caption depicted the gangster as scowling to the peace-loving, patriotic prisoners, "Now, let's hear who else wants to be repatriated."

This issue of screening nearly two hundred thousand prisoners to determine how many did *not* want repatriation to Communist rule tangled the armistice negotiations at the Korean village of Panmunjom, near Kaesong, and ignited eerie, bloody riots at the PW camps far to the south. A song about the situation (sung to the melody of "Without a Song") expressed our mood quite well:

> Without Kaesong
> The war would never end.
> Without Kaesong
> The strife would never mend.
> We'll spend our years
> Just crying in our beers
> Without Kaesong.
> We've our struggles and woe
> And sure as you know
> We've got a long tour.
> We've outdoor latrines;
> We're living on beans;
> We've got no *l'amour!*
> Without Kaesong . . .

The war had become a stalemate, a decisive end impossible without the kind of military action which might have boomeranged by enlarging the conflict. In the mammoth prisoner-of-war hospital, what seemed to us insane and fanatical behavior by thousands of Communist prisoner-patients was a reflection of the Korean situation as a

4

whole, and perhaps of the total world situation. If our PW hospital were to perform its mission of wholesale healing, we had to tolerate a situation which we regarded — from every aspect other than medical — as reprehensible and inhumane. We could have attempted to end all our difficulties with insulting, infuriating, insubordinate Communist patients by substituting shooting for talking. But any kind of suppression of sick and wounded prisoners of war, whatever the provocation, risked the support of our sixteen United Nations allies who had furnished at least token troops, the safety of our own prisoners and theirs and the sanctity of our moral position before world opinion.

American truce negotiations in Korea were hampered both by the voiding of MacArthur's threat to carry the war across the Yalu River into Manchuria, and by the humane, yet militarily and legally unprecedented decision that prisoners could refuse to return home. The Communists feared that even a single soldier refusing repatriation would constitute an embarrassing propaganda defeat. More than an internal problem, it had a potential impact upon the uncommitted nations in the Cold War. Yet the United Nations Command (in effect the United States) had no choice. Even were there no propaganda hay to be harvested, for even if every captive originally from Red territory wished to return home, there were still tens of thousands of forcibly impressed South Koreans in the PW total. Scores of innocent civilians were swept up in the changing tides of Communist advance and encirclement during the first months of the war. These Chinese "volunteers" also included many drafted anti-Communists (including former soldiers of Chiang Kai-shek), some of whom had, while behind our barbed wire, tattooed themselves with words and symbols expressing permanent defiance to Red rule. Deeper than skin-markings, prisoners of every ideological complexion displayed a fanaticism and hatred intensified by the corrosive effects of captivity. Prisoner riots were few but fierce. More frequent were the midnight kangaroo courts, which left bludgeoned bodies by a compound gate to be discovered at dawn.

Although we followed a policy of not jeopardizing armistice negotiations by drastic action toward the prisoners, or even by political indoctrination, the die-hard captives followed Communist orders regularly infiltrated to them. They had their own scarcely hidden but difficult to suppress indoctrination system. On one inspection tour of a compound of North Korean prisoners, I encountered a book-less and teacher-less class in session. One hut in ward #4 was filled far beyond bed capacity with patients far from bedfast. All of them had paper, crudely made writing brushes and ink surreptitiously made from tincture of gentian violet. Although it was clearly a classroom in operation, no "teacher" was visible, and it was obvious that none would be in sight as long as I was in the hut. Most patients were busy scratching Korean or Chinese characters, but some, I noticed, were writing in recognizable numbers, probably working out a mathematical problem. I asked what the "class" was learning. "Arithmetic, geography and communism," one unabashed "student" replied with a smile. We regularly discovered these informal classes, but seldom any teachers.

6

The workings of the Communist and Oriental-Communist mind and the difficulties of the Western mind in coping with such other-wordly logic and shrewdness, became apparent through the events at the crowded prison camps on the island of Koje and on the Korean mainland itself. Most of the able-bodied prisoners of war were held on Koje-do (Koje Island). The smaller mainland camp housed the rest, including newly captured prisoners, for whom it was a processing center and funnel channeling them to Koje-do. The nucleus of the mainland camp was an outsized army field hospital which handled all newly captured battle casualties. This facility also had the nearly overwhelming mission of treating all sick and injured from the PW population who were in need of definitive or lengthy treatment. In effect it was a mammoth general hospital, as far as we knew the largest (in bed capacity and occupied beds) in the world at that time.

The hospital's headquarters was the one permanent building, a two-storied, white-stuccoed school diverted from its purpose when survival displaced learning in Korea. Like a manor house of feudal days, it loomed over the camp's outbuildings—a dreary collection of huts and tents, surrounded by dusty villages and fecally aromatic rice paddies. Clustered next to the barbed-wire enclosed wards (several within each compound) were "worker's compounds" of able-bodied PW hospital laborers, ranging from captured doctors and nurses to the willing and unwilling hands who performed the thousands of housekeeping tasks each day.

The hospital had opened officially on the first day of September, 1950, as the "1st POW Field Hospital (Pro-

7

visional)." Its founding was during the period of the American break-out from the Taegu-Pusan foothold which was almost all of Korea that had not fallen to the Communists. Everything was provisional. It was difficult to distinguish friendly but fleeing South Korean troops from the enemy, and even more difficult to identify civilians from either. Soldiers trying to escape further action ripped off identifying garb and posed as refugees. The local government had to set up more than sixty camps to house the drifting population estimated at a quarter of a million people. To curtail guerrilla operations in the sector, UN forces were ordered to shoot anyone in civilian clothes seen moving at night.

Prisoners were being taken despite their efforts to confuse identities, because many were taken on the line, or found wounded—by American troops. Republic of Korea (ROK) soldiers seldom left enemy wounded alive. The first prisoners to arrive as patients could not wait for the official opening of the hospital. Several hundred who gathered in a nearby field were sprayed with DDT—as was the field—and a barbed wire fence strung. In ensuing days improvements were made. By the first of September, when there were 465 PW patients, a representative of the International Red Cross had inspected the facility. A week later a British Medical Corp officer with previous experience in the Orient came to offer advice. As always, the advice was to obtain what appeared to be unobtainable—in particular an X-ray unit. By September 14, when the patient population—mostly seriously wounded—had ballooned to 981 (including two PW women), the X-ray unit arrived, making care less primitive.

8

From all appearances the 1st POW Field Hospital
(Prov) was not an American camp. United States Army
staff, at a time when prisoners occupied every available
cot, consisted of two Medical Corps officers, one Army
Nurse Corps officer, one Medical Service Corps officer
and one enlisted man. The bulk of the medical staff consisted of eleven Korean doctors and twenty-two Korean
nurses. They all claimed medical training but there was
no time to check diplomas. In time many became profi-
cient via on-the-job training.

By mid-September army engineers were repairing the
battered "permanent" building: installing plumbing in
the former school so that surgery could be performed in-
doors and erecting a plaster-room for wholesale work on
casts. As they fanned out of their perimeter, American
forces were pinching off pockets of enemy troops and
sending more patients east and south. On October 5, the
hospital report noted, "The space available for patients
in tents and main hospital was filled to capacity today.
The POW Field Hospital Commander made a reconnaissance trip to look for more available space." The renam-
ing of the hospital (to remove the "provisional") became
effective the next day when 262 patients were admitted.
Twenty-four hours later another 392 arrived.

By the end of the year, seven thousand disabled prisoners crowded into the hospital. More than ten thousand
had already been treated and released, or had died. By
the time I arrived late in the summer of 1951, the hospital had already admitted nearly seventy thousand patients and, counting dead-on-arrival cases, had handled
nearly five thousand dead. Sometimes the dead mounted

9

so rapidly in front of the admissions hut that they had to be stacked like cordwood.

There was no way to take care of the immense load without prisoner help. This vast labor source was cheap but untrustworthy as many more able-bodied enemy were captured than wounded needing hospital care. Soon several enclosures were set up on the edge of the hospital camp to house the effectives. The structures also provided a place to which to discharge the reasonably healed or cured. In addition, it was inevitable that the war outside would eventually touch the crowded camps and that January it happened. A disabled plane crashed into Camp #3. There were thirty-seven dead-on-arrival at the hospital. In March, a trailer-truck overloaded with PW laborers tipped over into a rice paddy adding more DOAs.

Meanwhile the UN forces plunged north, sending over a hundred thousand more prisoners south. The winter was bitter, and hardship in the wards great; but by spring more than ten thousand patients lay in nearly a thousand tents. The first of 235 long semi-permanent huts were being built to accommodate the crush and provide protection from the weather.

Many patients were severe dysentery cases. In the first four months of 1951, there were more than twenty thousand dysentery admissions and, fortunately, no sudden increase in battle casualties. On March 23, 1951, when the hospital census had reached 10,834, there was a total daily turnover of 1,715 patients. For months thereafter admissions and discharges often exceeded a thousand PW patients a day. The twenty-five American army doctors had been augmented by a navy surgical team. Although

10

accustomed aboard to clean sheets and modern equipment, the new personnel quickly became efficient in the primitive camp.

The field hospital was a curious, mushrooming phenomenon. Amid the babel and chaos, often with improvised instruments, balky water supply, weak electricity, and drugs augmented by non-conforming supplies requested from civilian medical associates in the States, a motley collection of American and Korean doctors, nurses, pseudodoctors and alleged nurses provided the enemy with definitive, general hospital care, plus emergency treatment. Services included plastic and orthopedic rehabilitation and the fitting of dental, ocular, and upper and lower extremity prostheses. In fact, our intentions were too good. We were trying to provide care for everyone who needed it. Our eagerness swept up the friendly ailing as well as the enemy at a time when a wounded or sick civilian could obtain limited, if any, medical care in the teeming Korean hospitals. As a result we listed hundreds, then thousands of patients as PWs of South Korean origin, whether or not they had been, as many were, impressed into the Communist armies moving south.

Then too there were the families of "line crossers." There was no military rationalization to classify these dependents as prisoners of war. Yet in October, 1951, I admitted a father, mother and four children when no other facility would take them. They were undoubtedly North Koreans, but they were just as certainly noncombatants. Their hut had been shattered by an artillery shell and all but the three youngest children (all under five) were badly wounded. (Their medical evacuation tags read, "Dirty but well.")

The next day I received a call from the commanding general's aide telling me that he had heard we were harboring illegal patients and that we had to get rid of them. Using the army's own devices to stall, I agreed to investigate; and, while the three uninjured children played with a mounting pile of empty beer cans each day, we circumvented the order until mother, father, and ten-year-old daughter had all undergone surgery and post-operative care. For the girl it meant prosthetic assistance for an amputated gangrenous foot; for the mother a cast immobilizing pelvis and thighs; for the father only an arm in a sling. Of course the official investigation I had conducted had proved that the general was right, and (as he was notified) the family was immediately discharged—on paper. Two months later, they were actually released, all of them dressed in cut-down GI clothes. They had survived, but there was little to hope for in their future. For a while I wondered what had happened to them, but events made such memories quickly fade.

Humanitarian interests notwithstanding, the pressures on us to stop caring for civilian or ROK army wounded were great. Every South Korean "prisoner" was another potential combatant in the ideological civil war which went on in the wards behind the barbed wire, and this internal war for people's minds continued to result in dead and wounded left at the compound gates.

When possible, autopsies were performed on bodies where death had clearly occurred from something other than natural causes and the common clinical evidence seemed to suggest "execution" by application of a large blunt instrument to the head. We surmised a very blunt instrument indeed, because there was almost never any external bleeding, and never a murder weapon. But there were always plenty of sandbags around, and any of them might have been involved in the long succession of "perfect crimes." Another method was to try an already-condemned man in a PW "people's court" which was conducted at night when it was dangerous for UN personnel to be in the wards. The sentence often ordered the victim to become his own executioner. Hanging was the expected method and the body would not be cut down until we found it, in order to provide a grim deterrent to collaborationists or the politically unorthodox. Leaving a body hanging for such reasons was a common practice in South Korea. We saw one bridge far to the north, near the 38th parallel, where two guerrilla saboteurs had been caught while fixing explosives to the span. As soon as they surrendered, ROK soldiers hanged them from a girder where they swung for weeks—until picked nearly clean by carrion birds.

One hospital autopsy reported in the usual understated language that on 3 January 1952 a patient hospitalized for tuberculosis "was found dead hanging by the neck from a 60 cm rope." Hearsay evidence indicated that he had been accused of collaboration, threatened by the Communists and told to commit suicide in order to avoid being killed. He reportedly had tried to hang himself on 18 December, but failed. He was then sent for psychiatric examination but the NP evaluation was "not psychotic," and he was returned to his ward. We had sent him to his death. But, given the PW grapevine, he had already been among the living dead.

Sometimes the dead seemed to disappear. We would conclude that a missing PW was an escapee only to later find his body buried under a hut or a tent floor. It made autopsies difficult but "Spider," our chief pathologist, relished such cases and was obviously frustrated by being remote from a big-city police department morgue. Yet one case, he had to admit, was beyond anything in his experience—that of a PW who had drowned in feces. Naturally he first suspected foul play but the evidence indicated that the cause was our "eighth wonder of the world." In the hospital's largest ward was the biggest *benjo* (Japanese, I was told, for latrine) in history. It was a vast open facility of four hundred seats—or, rather, rectangular squatting holes—over "honey" pits fifteen to thirty feet deep. Given the endemic dysentery, what went in was always liquefied, and the surrounding vapor exceeded anything horror tales might offer. The PW, emaciated from illness, had been overcome by the fumes and fallen in. "Spider" discovered fecal material in the corpse's lungs and stomach. He *had* drowned.*

In the States I had been appalled by my first confrontation with military latrines—a dozen open porcelain toilets devoid of privacy, in a large room flanked by two troughs. Those conditions, however, were far superior to our largest PW hospital facility, where 400 stark holes screened

---

* In January, 1952 a dead PW was removed by his executioners in a large "honey-bucket." No one would have dreamed of examining the contents. My note about it, after the discovery, reads, "What a hearse!"

14

by a tarpaulin fence and open above to the weather, appeared to be dehumanizing in the extreme. All I could rationalize was that stoicism was a way of life in the East anyway.

A note I made in November 1951 suggested another of our problems in adjusting to behavior patterns foreign to the Western experience: "TB POW chewing on corpse in tent. Claims flesh of dead TB victim will cure his ailment." Nothing followed to indicate what we did about it but very likely nothing more that to remove the corpse. Nor did we remove the few long-haired young men who were pampered by PWs in every ward, although they were not physically sick. For most men who needed the opportunity, these were their women. It was better to look the other way and relieve a few PW tensions: the political unrest was trouble enough. Perhaps our tolerance indicated an end to some varieties of innocence. We could ignore a quarrel over the possession of a sleek, doe-eyed male but we tolerated only a certain level of murder.

In the first year, midnight executions and small-scale riots made the increasing prospect of civil war behind the barbed wire a deep concern for we had only a fraction of the manpower needed to contain it. As a result, identical messages were teletyped to medical clearing companies, MASHs (Mobile Army Surgical Hospitals) and other appropriate units:

RECENT REPORTS INDICATE INDISCRIM-
INATE DESIGNATION OF CIVILIANS COM-
MA COMMUNIST SYMPATHIZERS AND
ROK SOLDIERS AS PRISONERS OF WAR FOR

PURPOSES OF MEDICAL TREATMENT AND EVACUATION PERIOD UPON RECEIPT OF THIS MESSAGE STANDING OPERATING PROCEDURE WILL BE STRINGENTLY APPLIED AND INTERROGATION DURING MEDICAL EVACUATION WILL NOT REPEAT NOT CHANGE THE PATIENTS STATUS PERIOD PERSONNEL DESIGNATED AS PRISONERS OF WAR AND PLACED IN MEDICAL CHANNELS WILL RECEIVE REQUIRED MEDICAL CARE UNTIL SUFFICIENTLY RECOVERED TO PERMIT INTERNMENT IN A POW ENCLOSURE OR TRANSFER TO A POW HOSPITAL

Such procedures, however stringently applied, were not effective in the chaos of refugees, retreating soldiers and ROK deserters. To admit to being a civilian might mean no food and no care; to admit to being an enemy soldier might result in not being taken alive; and to confess to being a deserter from the South Korean army meant return to fighting or a firing squad. In any case few wanted to give their real names for fear of reprisals against families back home. We could not even be sure of the women in our custody, since many were Communist camp-followers or actual soldiers. Thus we devised a curious category eventually used in cases where the evidence warranted or when we were baffled: civilian internee. When truce talks began, these thousands of "misfits" became sore points in the negotiations because the

Communists wanted them all returned to North Korea. Indeed, one of the more difficult messages to respond to was:

REQUEST NUMBER OF SICK AND WOUND-
ED CIVILIAN INTERNEES ELIGIBLE FOR
REPATRIATION UNDER ARTICLE 110,
GENEVA CONVENTION 1949, WHOSE
FORMER RESIDENCE WAS NORTH OF THE
38TH PARALLEL

Would the information we could glean reflect any truth? We totted up the obviously erroneous data stored in the Quonset hut which held our Admissions and Dispositions records—a scrupulously neat chaos—and sent something forward, hoping that we would not be asked to produce a live body for every identification number.

With all its drawbacks, the PW hospital was far superior to anything the Republic of Korea had for treatment of its own sick and wounded soldiers. Yet Red propaganda directed toward the uncommitted nations and naive people everywhere called our medical facility a death camp where "many American doctors and scientists have come . . . on the pretext of rendering medical aid, but as eyewitnesses testify, they secretly experiment on living persons with the latest vaccines and chemical preparations, prepared for the murder of people." This accusation was an amazing example of twisting virtue into sin. Communist prisoners benefitted from the latest advances in medicine, anesthesia and surgery. They received the same quality of treatment as GIs received, although by necessity in a more primitive setting. The hospital was the "last resort" for a PW, while UN troops could be evacuated to Japan and to the States.

Institutional food there was unlike most other army hospitals. The PWs received a staple concoction of rice, cabbage, peppers, garlic and often some cut-up dried fish or squid cooked and served in fifty-five-gallon drums. Any variation in diet caused complaints, and the noisiest outbursts were reserved for meals prepared with Texas or Louisiana rice, for imported American rice was polished and considered unpalatable. To supplement their diet, the prisoners lured stray dogs (from what seemed an endless Korean canine population) into the wards, beat them to death and roasted them on makeshift spits. No one stopped the practice.

Hospital clothing was also unique. Every type of World War II surplus clothing descended upon us. With cold weather came electrically heated nylon flying suits. Unfortunately, the prisoners had no place to plug them in, and if they did they would have had to remain immobile. After some complaints, these suits were succeeded by officer-style long and short dress overcoats. Finally, except for the PW stencilling on each garment, the wards looked like the outdoors area of a shabby officer's club. Meanwhile American troops shivered in summer garb. Since their own cold-weather gear had not arrived, one by one they began pilfering the PW supplies for out-of-issue short dress overcoats not yet stencilled. I wore mine through two Korean winters. Often, when walking alongside the barbed-wire border at dusk, I wondered whether

I might be shot at by an itchy-fingered sentry who mistook me for an escaping prisoner.

Patient care was expert when we could figure out what was wrong. Wounded prisoners presented no diagnostic problem, but sick ones did. The first words of Chinese I learned as an admissions officer were a recognizable equivalent to "Where is your pain?" This was not conclusive, for the patient could have been a malingerer or what spy stories would call an *agent provocateur*, infiltrating the system. Interpretation difficulties compounded the problems. A doctor performed his ward rounds, or worked at the admissions hut, in tandem with Korean and Chinese PW interpreters. Sometimes a knot of PWs and PW interpreters would gather round the cot and argue — with gesticulations added — over the proper explanation of the patient's symptoms. The American doctor simply stood by, bewildered by the unintelligible chattering. Frequently the solution would be to order an X-ray. If it proved nothing, the PW would be returned to the work force, having — in some cases — already delivered his message.

In April, 1952, the war in Korea was almost two years old. While truce negotiations dragged on, the bloody seesaw continued through yet a third year of conflict. The lethargy of hopelessness, alternating with the rising tensions of hope, compounded both our frustrations and the unrest among the prisoners. Some of this turmoil is recorded in a pile of scratch-pad jottings I made at the time, some of them detailed and leisurely, others sketched fragmentarily in the haste of the moment. In large measure they represent notes for letters home which for security or personal reasons, I never wrote as graphically, if at all. In sum, they chronicle one of the most fantastic minor episodes in the Korean struggle from the perspective of a green young administrative officer at the hospital camp. The young officer was greener than most. A thoroughgoing civilian, he acquired a "direct" commission under army regulations—soon afterwards tightened up considerably—which gave lieutenant's bars to qualified young scientists, including those with any Bachelor of Science degree. (Mine was in education.) His active duty experience prior to Korea consisted of six weeks' training, some of which proved useful. He learned how to salute, for example; and to respect firearms by learning how to fire a rifle in a direction generally away from him. Best of all, he crawled on his belly under fire several times as part of the traditional infiltration course which taught that preservation and panic were incompatible. But most of his training turned out to be the on-the-job variety, based upon that most effective of motivations, necessity.

What follows, with names altered and certain other details juggled to preserve the privacy of individuals as much as possible, is a thirty-eight-day segment of my notes, refurbished in grammar, and expanded from shorthand fragments where necessary for clarity. The facts and reflections—each from a thoroughly subjective and limited perspective—are neither altered nor post-judged. The notes have been kept in their original first-person and the present tense in order to preserve the flavor of immediacy which, as I look over these daily segments more than two decades later, makes them appear to be written by someone whom I once knew well, but with whom I have been out of touch for a long time.

That very young lieutenant is a revelation of how naive and untrained an officer can be, yet somehow manage to function reasonably successfully within situations for which the army could not have prepared him anyway. We have not progressed very far since then, having fought a longer and more frustrating war in Vietnam. Again American innocence was a victim as we seem unable to imagine the extent and depth of communist tenacity and duplicity. Nor have we been able to comprehend why people whose territory we have fought over in their ostensible protection do not always appreciate our presence. Experience is a poor teacher for the next generation: one seems to need to learn from one's own mistakes, even when that learning comes too late.

The American army was unprepared for Korea. Soft after the Japanese occupation and debilitated by postwar cutbacks, it was quickly beefed-up with inadequate reservists and hastily trained draftees, few of whom could find any patriotic fervor in their souls. Ironically, inadequate officers and men frequently were detailed to the handling of prisoners of war, a delicate job needing — especially in the case of Communists — the most experienced and subtle minds. The enlisted men on PW duty were often rejects of one kind or another. They were augmented at the prisoner-of-war hospital by draftees assigned as medics because of their conscientious objections to carrying firearms.

Medical officers were flagrantly the least military of all. Pressured into accepting a commission by the overly fair doctor-draft law, they had little interest in military service and no enthusiasm for military discipline. I can recall one M.D. strolling down a post street at Fort Sam Houston, Texas, in the summer of 1951, wearing parts of two different types of uniforms, and white tennis shoes. He was halted by a military policeman obviously accustomed to such phenomena and courteously but firmly escorted back to his quarters to change clothes.

The result of staffing a huge, sprawling, tumultuous prisoner-of-war hospital with personnel many of whom were counting the days until discharge, and had no strong feelings about "causes," leads me to wonder how we came through the conflict with even a draw.

For the PW hospital, the most violent phase of the Korean War began in April, 1952. It was, by standards of modern, push-button warfare, a small, shabby affair, of short duration — however long it seemed. Nevertheless, although much about war contains the same ratio of the prosaic and the nightmarish, few battles were ever fought on such unusual terms. The young Joyce Cary once wrote a memoir of the 1912 Balkan war in which he served with an English Red Cross unit. In it he concluded, "If this proves a disappointing book it must be because there is too much eating, and too little incident in it — too much like life, which is perhaps disappointing for the same reason."

It did not seem like too little incident then.

April 15, 1952–April 30, 1952

Took the dusty ride to Pusan this morning, with Sgt. Klinghoffer driving as usual—which means at top speed, without regard for road conditions. And as usual, careened around dozens—it seems—of fragrant, agonizingly slow "honey" carts, whose drivers pay no more attention to us than their oxen do. The rush is partly to get past the smell and partly to get one of our officers who is being transferred to a line unit to a train that is supposed to leave at noon, but probably never does. He's been with us only since January but is grateful to leave. When the jeep pulls up to the Pusan RTO, he leaps out, even before we've stopped. After waiting for Klinghoffer to turn off the ignition he grabs his duffel bag with one hand, shakes mine with the other, and dashes off with the shout, "No need to hold my hand until the cattle car leaves. So long!"

The clock on the stubby red-brick RTO steeple strikes twelve, and Klinghoffer automatically looks up at it, then adjusts his World War Two-vintage service-model Elgin. A ragged boy runs up, his nose almost touching the watch crystal.

"Buy your watch, Sar-gint?"

"*Carra!*" Klinghoffer screams, and swings his arm free. (He's been victimized before, selling a new PX watch for a roll of paper with one legitimate bill on top.) The boy darts away with a grin.

Several more urchins swarm toward us, dragging shoe-

25

shine boxes in the mud. No sale. Where we are, shined shoes are ridiculous.

A truck backs into the empty spot next to us. A bedraggled boy, his bare feet and his shoeshine box both in a large mud puddle, is busy with the problem of guiding the Army vehicle via his gratuitous advice to inch back a little at a time. *"Skoshi, skoshi,"* he calls; but the driver has been here before, and ignores him and the pedestrians.

A siren whines. No one looks up. An Army ambulance is making its regular run to meet the hospital train. One white-goateed Korean, bent by the loaded A-frame on his back, moves slowly out of the ambulance's way. The children scatter in front of it, as if playing a game, then head for the circle in the RTO square, and sprawl under the few scrawny trees.

There are five emaciated trees. Rags, tattered clothes, and bits of string hang from their branches, making them look like grotesque, out-of-season Christmas trees. Under them—in spite of the children—people in rags sleep, eat, chatter, or stare in silence. Around the square others are buying and selling, begging and bartering. The sight has a sickening fascination for me. Little children selling stolen American cigarettes or imitation Parker 51 pens, replenishing their stock by deftly pickpocketing a GI while offering to sell him something. Beggars accosting each well-dressed passer-by. (The beggar boys, I'm told, have a Faginlike chieftain who preys on them, beats them for poor production, takes away a percentage of their gains.)

A prosperous Korean businessman in smart gray hat

26

An old papa-san.

and blue topcoat strolls by, as if the tumult doesn't exist. Just behind him a wild tangle of hair appears. The stench is overpowering. A grimy leper, with mottled face and hands rotted away to raw stumps, has come begging, silently. "He's a regular here," says Klinghoffer. "Haven't you ever seen him before, sir? Usually sleeps in the circle. *Carra!*"

The leper turns slowly away. He had been placed in a Korean leper colony, but retraced his steps each time to the RTO, his adopted home. Some morning here he won't wake up.

Through the confusion an old *papa-san* strolls by haughtily, with black top hat (and chin strap), white baggy trousers and coat, long-stemmed pipe, and sparse black beard. A throwback to the Korea of old. Trailing behind him is a thin shaft of smoke.

There's some hubbub to the left of our jeep. An UNCACK (U. N. Civil Assistance Command, Korea) 1951 Dodge, still glisteningly new, is slumped down with a flat tire. (It occurs to me that I've never seen a real 1952-model car—only in magazine ads.) The Korean driver has a dilemma: he doesn't know how to operate the jack, and buzzing around him are little ragged "coaches." He knows that if he goes for help and leaves the car unattended, every movable part will be gone when he comes back. Incongruously nearby are Korean cars, strange, hybrid monstrosities which resemble wire-and-tape resurrections of the contents of Japanese and American junk heaps. Wheezing and grunting, they scatter some children who look like animated GI blankets. Barely heard, a horn bleats futilely—an Army jeep bearing a placard, "U. S. Mail: Do Not Delay." It waits behind the rattletraps.

The circle grows more crowded. Women in dirty rags held together by GI blankets tied around their waists by pieces of string. Women and children with crying babies and smiling babies lashed to their backs with rags or strips of blanket. Children carry brothers and sisters hardly larger than themselves wrapped to their backs. Little children bare from the waist down slip in and out of the crowd. A woman nurses her baby by shifting the infant around in his cocoon from back to front—and then opening her dirty black blouse. Her baggy trousers are a mass of rags and patches. The baby is content; the faint wind plays with his hair, ruffling it as he suckles.

One mother shifts uneasily, jostling the child on her back. The reason becomes evident rapidly: a wet stain is becoming larger. Quickly she sets him down and unwinds the mummylike layers of rags around him. The damp rags get hung on the tree to her left, and the child joins the other bare-bottomed toddlers in the square. Nearby a woman squats, holding her infant aloft by his haunches as he relieves himself through the conveniently engineered split in the seat of his pants. The placid expression on the baby's face is absurd.

The RTO clock strikes twelve-thirty. Although it is bright midday, there are still families with all their possessions on their backs sleeping soundly all around the square. In and out among the huddled groups springs a square-faced Korean with iron-gray hair. He walks on all fours, with catlike agility. He has stumps which end at the thighs for legs.

In a corner of the RTO square a group of smartly dressed "Sears Roebuck girls" keep apart from the lower classes. Superficially they appear to be momentary glimpses of the States, outfitted as they are in American mail-order clothes (by the GIs who keep them), even to the nylons on pedestals of high heels.

In the roadway around the circle, and in and out among the parked vehicles like ours, treads a boy in tattered green Army fatigues. A larger boy of eleven or twelve walks behind him, stooped slightly, his hand on the shoulder of the smaller, who is carrying an empty, dirt-encrusted half-gallon paint can in one hand and a blackened tablespoon in the other. It's obvious that the older one is blind, and obvious why from the roughly healed shrapnel gashes in his shaven scalp.

"Hello, hello," the smaller one pleads, at once exhausting his meager English vocabulary, and falling silent for a moment. "Hello, hello."

American uniforms are suddenly all around. Knots of GIs just off the boat from Japan or the train from Seoul are taking snapshots. One of the women nursing a baby turns her back.

The armed soldiers debarking from a six-by-six truck are swarmed over by children, and try to elbow through them. Some GIs hesitate, but a corporal buys their freedom by taking several chocolate bars from his pockets and throwing them about ten yards, into the roadway. A path opens as the kids scatter after the red-and-white candy bars.

"O.K., Klinghoffer," I say. The first words we've exchanged in half an hour. "Ready to go back now? I think

31

I've built up enough immunity to face our place for a while."

By 1400 hours we're back behind our barbed wire and scrounge late lunches.

There are some PW death certificates to sign, and the Admissions and Dispositions hut to check, but little to encourage thoughts of my indispensability.

At 1545, without preliminary warning to officers at the hospital—although we knew it was coming very soon —the PW afternoon labor details are ordered to return to their residence compounds, leaving work from road grading to honey-bucket emptying in the middle of things. While the PWs are still in transit, we can see, in the distance, the long-anticipated sound truck with portable generator-trailer rolling into the camp enclosure. Making a left turn past the nearest PW compounds, the truck halts at the main gate of compound ONE (surgical patients and resident PW ward attendants). The ambulatory patients inside ONE gather expectantly by the gate to watch the setting-up of the loudspeaker unit and listen to the curious vocabulary of sound-testing. More puzzling to them is the long silence which follows, while the truck's personnel loll about, now and then looking at their watches.

At 1730, finally, after all wards—as usual—have been emptied of their UN personnel for the night, a recorded message is blared into the compound that all prisoners of war, hospitalized and able-bodied, will be "screened" beginning the next day, to determine who wish to return to North Korea and China, and who would *forcibly resist repatriation.* They are told that they will

have the night to think it over; but they have had many
nights to think it over already, for screening is underway
on Koje-do, and—without our telling them—they know
it.

None of the doctors, and few of the GIs, filing out of
the compound, stay for the performance. It's dinnertime.

The PWs listen undemonstratively to the statement,
broadcast successively in Korean, Chinese, and English
—the last for us, I suppose. It includes a pledge from
Communist representatives at Panmunjom that there will
be no retaliation against the anti-Communists who wish
to return home—even those Nationalist Chinese (I assume) with their flamboyantly tattooed pro-Chiang
Kai-shek or anti-Communist slogans. In English the message was lullingly pacific:

> *"We wholeheartedly welcome the return of all of
> our captured personnel to the arms of the mother-
> land; we have further guaranteed, in an agreement
> reached with the other side, that all captured per-
> sonnel shall, after their repatriation, rejoin their
> families to participate in peaceful construction and
> live a peaceful life."*

Further, the PWs are reminded to think of their families and friends back home—that if they chose *not* to be
repatriated, they would face a life in which they could
be sure of nothing but hardship, and they would probably never see their families or homes again. For us to
supplement the Communist message by couching the
PWs' choice in such terms, and to insist that only those
who vowed that they would "forcibly resist repatriation"

would be permitted to remain, seems our attempt to provide the principle of voluntary repatriation but not to encourage its wholesale use. This could possibly leave too many prisoners on our hands, as well as lose face for the Communists and thus impair prospects for a peace settlement.

Only in the sullenness etched upon their faces is any emotion expressed. As the sound truck prepares to move to the next compound, knots of PWs drift silently into their huts, as if the news had come as no surprise. When the statement is blared into TWO, the reaction of the PWs is the same. In THREE we see a change: the prisoners walk away from the announcement immediately after it begins; but the unimpressed loudspeakers blare on at the unseen audience, huddled in the huts.

In each successive compound we get the same quiet results, and the only sounds are the garbled echoings of the loudspeaker's message. Since news of bloody riots over screening in Koje has been our main topic of conversation, we are surprised at the placid reaction. The news is no secret kept from the PWs, for the bulk of our admissions in the last few days—several hundred—have been new "battle" casualties for whom the battle supposedly had been over some time ago. These were PWs from the new "front" in the camp at Koje, both Communist and anti-Communist in sympathy, most of them not seriously injured but in total too many for the small hospital on the island to handle. Still, we expect all of the screening here to take about five days.

Just as we are about to wind up the day's business of admissions, transfers, and discharges, a report comes to me by GI messenger that immediately prior to the screening announcement a Chinese PW patient who had been missing from his bed for five days has been found alive. He was hiding under the floorboards of a Quonset hut in ONE, existing only on the water which seeped through. He hid there, he said, because he doesn't want to be returned to Red China, and nearly succeeded in ensuring his nonreturn via exposure and malnutrition. His anxiety over the prisoner exchange seems premature: most inhabitants of ONE, in fact, are carrying on routine housekeeping tasks in the twilight, after a brief sulk in the huts.

Enough prisoners seem busy with their favorite pastime—knitting—to alleviate any serious worry for us. If they're not trading blankets after dark, they're finding new uses for them in daylight. Barbed-wire fences and ROK tower and perimeter guards seem to be neither deterrent nor handicap to the cover-of-night transactions with helpful villagers of "blankets, wool, O.D." for dried fish, *sake,* or other contraband. The result is that Korea is now both drab and olive-drab. The South Korean civilian population uses blankets for everything: insulates huts with them; uses them for shawls, rugs, and mattresses; unravels the blankets to knit socks and sweaters and underwear; cuts them up to fashion trousers, breeches, jackets, skirts, and such. Every well-dressed Korean is indebted to the blanket, from the infant bound to *mama-san's* back by a strip of O.D. blanket to the aged, goat-bearded *papa-san,* smoking his long-stemmed pipe while sitting cross-legged on his luxurious O.D. rug.

If they don't sell their blankets (and then complain that they were stolen so they can get a new issue), the PWs pass the time by knitting clothes out of the blankets they unravel. When they run out of their own stock they steal from bedridden, defenseless patients close at hand, knowing we'll replace those. Bodies in the morgue are often found sans clothes and blankets, although clad and covered on arrival. Sometimes we find them nude and dead in the wards, completely unidentified, and have to rely on matching fingerprints. Recently a new squad-tent was erected in one compound but wasn't ready for occupancy when darkness made it necessary for the tent crew to pull out. The next morning the crew returned and found little left of the tent but a few scattered wooden pegs. The neighboring PWs were placidly knitting garments from the improvised yarn.

But blankets are a crucial unit of exchange. Most commodities are price-fixed according to their worth in blankets. Sometimes a PW is actually caught marketing his blanket. The penalty: exile to Koje-do. We probably haven't seen all the possible PW uses for the O.D. blanket yet; or all the possible civilian uses.

Often the Koje exile manages to return, usually via a borrowed positive chest X ray, and re-enters the blanket business. For the most part we've put a stop to blanket peddling on the part of PWs who feign mental illness to get admitted: the psycho ward has no fence bordering on the exterior of the enclosure. Sometimes even the authentically sick can be found on a cold, gray morning strolling to the chow line with only a blanket covering an emaciated frame, like a limp tent on a pole.

36

He's sold his clothes to someone who's sold his blanket "over the fence" for half the proceeds of the blanket transaction (four fish). The next day he may have sold his own blanket for a bottle of *sake*, only to find out what he already suspected—that although *sake* keeps one warmer than a blanket, its effect is only temporary. Then he comes to dinner, huddled in a throng of clothed companions for warmth, clad only in rice bowl and chopsticks. An angry GI will pull him out of line and ask him whether he has a blanket, with a threat of exile in his voice:

"Blanket have-a-no."

"Koje-do!"

It is an unwitting Gilbert-and-Sullivanesque bit of repartee—a macabre *Mikado*. A few weeks or months later the PW is back again under another name, this time, perhaps, faking epilepsy. The business ends the same way:

"Have-a-no."

"Koje-do!"

It's a frustrating cycle, but at least the knitting and tailoring indicate that the situation's relatively normal.

Dusk fades into darkness by the time the loudspeaker trucks have made their circuit of the passive compounds. A quiet night, except that tanks and half-tracks clatter and rumble back and forth along the perimeter roads, when up to now they've been mainly for display purposes.

Before breakfast, reports of last night's activity inside the compounds come in by GI messenger and telephone. They're hardly necessary, for on the way up the hill to mess we see a number of PWs by the barbed-wire fences, smilingly displaying ominous evidence of a night of coercion. Apparently in the seclusion of their tents and huts, Communist leaders in the compounds held meetings in which PWs were forced to sign their names in blood to documents stating that all prisoners wish to be repatriated, and will refuse interrogation. In SIX, some PWs, possibly trying to avoid this kind of intimidation, tried climbing out, ripped their flesh on the barbed wire in their anxiety to escape, and managed only to disappear into the adjacent compound THREE. We'll find them when we screen THREE—which is already loud with Communist songs, although it is barely daybreak.

Two additional ambulance platoons (twenty-four ambulances) arrive to augment our own large supply. For moving screened patients from one ward to another we'll need all of them. They will also augment our trucks which will be moving nonpatients.

At 0630, PWs in the interior workers' compound (SEVEN) are aroused and moved out quietly to join prisoners in the exterior nonpatient compounds. The operation goes smoothly, interrogation rapid. Those PWs desiring repatriation "North" are directed to walk away from the screening tent one way, those wanting to stay "South" go the other way, thus ensuring freedom of choice and segregation of groups. Only about 25 per cent (much smaller than the first ratios reported from Koje) screen South. Those choosing to be repatriated—seventeen hundred North Koreans in this first batch—are loaded on trucks for shipment to Koje. As the heavily guarded convoy begins to move, the Communists aboard begin to sing (in Korean), "We've won the victory; now we're going home." They wave hundreds of (somehow) previously hidden North Korean and hammer-and-sickle flags as the convoy—noisy, colorful, and embarrassing—moves through the enclosure and out, down the main road to the port. The spectacle is a sorry one for frustrated Americans and South Koreans to observe, for the demonstration is tolerated by the American armed escort, under orders to avoid any incidents.

The news from Koje is hardly any better, mainly consisting of reports of anarchy in some compounds there. We expect an eventual influx of prisoner casualties from Koje, for the Communists there seem bent on continuing resistance to screening—to prevent any PWs from choosing South.

The morning processing in the two exterior workers' compounds is so rapid that the estimates of how long it will take to screen the patients (whose physical problems will necessarily slow us down) become more optimistic. After all, the able-bodied have more potential for troublemaking than the bedridden. And interrogated without incident are 2350 PWs. The slightly better than six hundred who elect to stay South are returned to one of the compounds they left, and watch the line of tank-guarded trucks pull away.

We move down to TWO to assist in the removal of eighty patients on our preliminary list of those too seriously ill to be questioned about screening, or too incompetent mentally to make a rational decision. When these are being borne out on litters to the shuttling ambulances—even before we can be sure we have *all* the worst cases out, especially from the neuropsychiatric ward, the PW compound monitors block the beginning of screening. Using their bodies as barricades, the monitors and their henchmen physically block the tent and hut entrances and exits, and declare that the prisoners in TWO have no wish to be screened. Since the American military policemen there to supervise traffic to the screening tent at the gate may not employ force, they stand helpless, waiting for the first PW.

The anti-Communists in the compound are apparently intimidated into inaction. No PW comes forward, and the compound *honcho's** declaration stands up in the silence. Then the shouting, flag-waving convoy of PW laborers comes into view high on the hilly road above the camp. Inspired, five PWs in compound TWO clamber to the roof of a hut and raise their own North Korean flag, fixing it firmly to the roof by its improvised flagpole, obviously a former litter pole. As soon as the flag, with its big red star, unfurls in the wind, great cheering goes up from the PWs, and American personnel prudently begin exiting from the compound.

At 1430 the Communists obey an order to haul the flag down, but refuse to give it up—or to continue the

honcho: PW "boss" (spokesman-leader, representing ruling PW clique)

40

interrupted screening operation. Instead, the PW chief *honcho* threatens the M.P. officers on the other side of the fence that more than fifty prisoners whose sympathies the PWs know to be South are being held as hostage— until we let Communist prisoners supervise the screening. The parleying is impassioned and prolonged, and a few PWs use the opportunity of the confusion to manage the risky escape over the fences to safety, while sympathetic ROK tower guards look on. The weather is helping the escapees—it's been violently windy and dusty all day. Clouds of dust obscure everything now. It all looks and seems unreal.

No progress. The PWs in TWO won't budge from the compound or permit themselves to be interrogated there. Still, the camp Commanding Officer refuses to force the issue, and forbids any attempt at forcible movement from TWO, even if we euphemistically declare that it's for medical reasons.

A sudden loss of interest in TWO occurs because of a diversion in THREE, where two flags suddenly go up. Lt. Anderson, in charge there, isn't pleased, but the same orders about no force apply to him too. No choice left, he orders all his men to evacuate the compound, while the bright red-and-purple flags, with a red star in a white circle, ripple in the wind, flouting our prestige as well as our discipline. There was never much real discipline on Koje, but I don't remember anything like this *here* before today.

On the far side of the camp, meanwhile, our batting average is improving a little. The compound of female prisoners is processed quickly and without incident, then hastily divided in two—North and South—by a double barbed-wire fence. They watch quietly until it's all over, and then hundreds gather on the North side, by the thin new separating fence and sing Red Army songs at the South women. It gets windier, dustier, and darker, but the women huddle by the barbed wire and scream at each other.

Nurse Major Evelyn Smith tries to enter THREE to reason with her Chinese friends and pulls rank on a green new lieutenant who orders her away. After a shouting contest she leaves, threatening to see that the lieutenant is court-martialled for disobeying a superior officer. She would only have been killed, or held as hostage, he explains to me. But I tell him that Evelyn completely lacks a sense of fear, and thinks she's a man—except when she's in bed with one. She was brought up in China, daughter of a medical missionary, and speaks the language like a native. The Chinese PWs in orthopedic surgery think she's great, and she lavishes affection on them while they take advantage of her to acquire contraband. Strange habits for a female whose life has been spent in hospitals. She never seems to wash, has ragged, yellowed, smoker's teeth and the dirtiest fingernails I've seen apart from gas station attendants and coal miners, and has the most unladylike vocabulary imaginable. Yet some femaleness shows through—curves that combat fatigues can't hide, and luminous brown eyes which overwhelm a gaunt, sallow face.

Most nurses are staying far away from the fences, having been ordered not to go into any wards, even safe ones. Only those on operating room and post-op duty have anything to do. But there are no orders to evacuate any nurses.

Late afternoon. A romantically foolhardy "military" operation is carried out in THREE—reminiscent of a bygone age when a battle flag meant a good deal. Unarmed GIs from THREE's staff, led by an indignant Lt. Anderson, enter the compound through the main gate and tear down the Red flags flying impudently from the two huts. The Communist prisoners mass about them, heaving rocks and swinging clubs. Almost surrounded, they manage to break out and retreat through the compound to the adjacent gate of SIX, on the far side. When ROK soldiers, bayonets fixed, rush into the compound THREE sally-port at the opposite end, the GIs escape into SIX, where all is remarkably quiet. Casualties are two GIs beaten—nothing serious. This is the first time I can recall armed men ever entering a PW compound here.

Lt. Anderson feels sheepishly triumphant about the escapade because he's managed to rescue his "statue." He had had an artistically minded PW orthopedic technician in THREE make him a bust of himself out of casting plaster, and was so pleased with the result that he kept it in the compound admissions hut where he could admire it regularly. But he was afraid to take it "home" to his hut because he was sure that the predominantly M.D. occupants of "Bedside Manor" (the sign above our door) would laugh at him. They've seen it and laughed anyway, and have christened it "Narcissus." Now Andy's taken his statue—wrapped up in a blanket —back to the hut and locked it inside the wooden chest he keeps next to his sack. The bust (we had all seen it while it was in the compound) stands about eighteen inches high and looks strikingly like Anderson, except that "Narcissus's" eyes have a decidedly Oriental slant.

We deliberately pay no attention to the bust or to its new hiding place. It's obvious from Andy's bewildered expression that he can't understand our lack of curiosity. After his whirlwind dash through THREE, the continuing trouble there may seem nothing extraordinary to him, but it occupies the rest of us, for that compound is now out of control.

After the ROKs exit from THREE, the PWs begin massing in THREE's large recreation area: workers, aid-men, and ambulatory orthopedic patients, some dragging plaster-encased limbs, hundreds on crutches. With shouts and sweeping arm movements, the PW leaders incite the mob, drawing more and more PWs into the vortex and sustaining them in frenzied singing and shouting. "Victory! Victory!" they chant in Korean. "We won the war and we want to go home!" Tiring of that, they roar the North Korean Army anthem alternately with the victory shout. Hearing the singing carried on the fierce wind, other compounds join in. The chant grows louder and echoes back from the hills, eerie as it blends dissonantly with the howling and whistling of the rising wind. Fascinated, I watch alone from the plateau above the compound, while dust clouds obscure the sunset and early twilight settles. Suddenly I realize that I've had no dinner and will have to scrounge something from the mess officer.

By early evening the total of anti-Communist escapees

from TWO (aided by dust clouds and understanding ROK guards) numbers sixty. More are believed trapped within, not permitted by the Communist monitors to use the excuse of needing medical treatment to get to the security of the sally-port. But there still seems no likelihood that the demonstrations or the disobedience will be put down by force. The command attitude seems to be that the PWs will eventually simmer down when they see that they gain nothing except disruption of their medical care. Then they'll permit themselves to be screened—without a repetition of the Koje nonsense of a few days ago.

There is loud singing in the compounds at night, and some screams are heard above the wind, making us wonder whether the choral practice is a cloak for kangaroo courts. Matter-of-factly, one body is brought to the gate by the PWs in THREE. There are no marks of violence, and "Spider" Biddle, routed from the sack, hastily diagnoses probable sandbagging on the back of the head and neck. Other PWs in THREE break through into SIX to murder another PW. He'd let the GIs (who took the flags down in THREE) escape by helping to keep the gate open between the compounds; and he is hanged in full view of the PWs on the plateau above in FOUR —who tell us. Since the ROK tower guards apparently may not shoot unless the PWs attempt to break *out* (not into another compound), they take their instructions literally and remain silent onlookers. Meanwhile the murderers return to THREE and merge with the mob.

The effect in SIX is electric. Two hundred and forty-

45

four anti-Communist PWs, mostly TB patients, fearing a more immediate threat to their lives than bacilli, mass at the outer gate in SIX and plead for refuge elsewhere —"while there is still time," one appeals. M.P. guards open the gate and escort them to temporary haven in ELEVEN, just emptied of Koje-bound laborers. No effort is made by the Communist leadership in SIX to stop the flight. No *honchos* even in sight.

TWO is still closed—refuses screening unless its PW monitors handle it themselves. At ONE, the officer in charge of the screening team is met at the gate by the PW *honcho* (who can speak and understand a good deal more English than he pretends) and his battle-blinded interpreter. Succinctly, in the three-way conversation between *honcho*, interpreter, and American officer—not all of which I could catch—the PW spokesman leaves no room for negotiation or for face-saving twists in the screening procedure:

"There will be no screening in this compound. We are all going back home."

"If that's so, then all PWs in your compound will have the opportunity to state this, so that we can enter their names on a list to be sent to your army's representatives."

"This is unnecessary and contrary to international law. We think that your so-called screening is illegal and a violation of the Geneva Convention, which intends that every prisoner of war be permitted to go home."

"But your government did not sign the Geneva Convention."

"We were not an independent nation when the Convention was ratified. We were under the imperialist domination of your new ally, Japan."

"You haven't signed it since!"

"Nevertheless we believe that you, as a signatory,

47

should certainly abide by it. A PW has the right to go home."

"But if he doesn't want to return . . ."

"There is no provision in the Convention for that—only that it is the responsibility of each side to return the prisoners it has taken. You cannot take it upon yourselves to rewrite international law."

"But it would be the same as signing a death warrant, wouldn't it, to force PWs with tattooed anti-Communist markings to return?"

"No. We are a forgiving people and understand that these PWs were forced to submit to this torture, so you Americans would have a pretext to raise the screening issue. But you are not to blame: it is Wall Street, and its traitor puppet in Korea, Syngman Rhee. Haven't you broadcast into all the wards the official statement of our peace negotiators that all PWs are welcomed back to their homelands?"

"Yes, but many PWs say that they will resist to the death being returned—that they wish to begin new lives on this side of the thirty-eighth parallel."

"We will resist your illegal screening to the death!"

With that, confident in the irrefutable logic and essential humanity of his position, the *honcho,* hand upon his interpreter's shoulder to guide him, strides back to harangue those of his comrades who could not hear—or follow—the English-Korean colloquy. Cheers come up from the crowd of PWs, while we stand helplessly on the other side of the sally-port gate; and all we can do is mutter to each other about the Geneva Convention's having been codified in the idealistic days when no one could have imagined captured troops not wanting to return home, and its now being turned upon us in Frankenstein fashion.

One of the PWs in the crowd, we can see, has an O.D. blanket which, with the aid of a partner, he stretches out full width so that a neat English lettering job (in white) can be seen: "PW EVER READY TO SACRIFICE LIVES IN COURAGEOUS FIGHT . . ." The remainder rapidly disappears from sight. Spotted by the *honcho*, the PW pair are angrily ordered by scowls and gesticulations to put the defiant slogan under wraps, having, in their eagerness, exposed it prematurely. They hastily crumple it into a bundle, then weave into the mob and lose themselves, while their compound spokesman's speech goes on, unbroken.

The *honcho* is a formerly quiet man, a minor battle casualty among many serious surgical cases, almost all battle casualties too. Under him the PW ward attendants are running things smartly. Some of them are the demagogic soapbox orators who used to lead compound rallies demanding better food, labor conditions, and medical care. At home such agitation might have led them to a firing squad, but in our hands they argue that we don't follow the Geneva Convention, when in general they've never been better fed or had better medical care in their lives. Our mistake. Few of them had ever heard of Geneva until we righteously posted the Convention regulations—in Korean and Chinese—in each compound. After that they would gather around the documents and assess each article to determine how closely we adhered to the letter, rather than the principle, of the agreement. Of course the Communists ignore Geneva as far as we can tell about our men held prisoner.

SIX and THREE are temporarily like one compound, with the gates between them open and some PWs running back and forth. No GIs enter THREE, but some go into SIX when the prisoners there finally (as a hint that they want medical treatment restored) close the connecting gates. More than a thousand far-advanced tuberculosis cases are in SIX and need continuing care, but not much can be chanced.

It has been dark as twilight since 0900—a gray brown veil draped over the area. Although we suspect that there's business for him there, I refuse to let my morgue clerk and his detail enter any compounds to check. "Digger" is blasé about the danger that he might become a hostage or get hurt ("As far as I'm concerned, sir, the biggest danger around here is TB."). But the hospital has nearly ceased to be a hospital. All but emergency surgery is halted, and medical treatment is almost impossible. Most doctors are sitting listlessly in their huts by tall bottles of Japanese beer, and there is a sudden resurgence of interest in bridge, attended by acrimonious arguments ("I'll bet you wouldn't even talk to your wife like that!").

In the afternoon, American medical officers chance a re-entry into SIX. Communist PW Dr. Chung and Mr. Shi, the PW X-ray technician there (a former teacher in Pyongyang) greet the American doctors with smiles but also with a firm English "Now we're in charge here." And Mr. Shi adds the demand to know the hut and tent locations of the 224 escaped anti-Communists as the

50

price of permitting the restoration of medical treatment.
Refusing the demand, Capt. Al Griffith then turns to
another *honcho* in the greeting party and inquires about
the disposition of the executed gate monitor. Politely
smiling, the *honcho* quips, "We don't know. Maybe he
was buried, but I wouldn't know where." Emboldened
by the private joke, the PW doctor demands access to
medicines on his own and is coldly refused. "We can't
practice medicine under these conditions," says Griff
as formally as if he were at the converted teahouse at
Kaesong or the hut at Panmunjom; and, following him,
the American personnel turn and stalk out, M.P. sally-
port guards locking the gate again from the outside.

Anti-Communists are reported in charge in FIVE, having beaten a North Korean major (PW) who attempted
to instigate an uprising there. Thereafter all is quiet. So
far (1400 hours) TWO's rations for the day are undelivered (it had been held up in the hope that non-
delivery would encourage a screening agreement). When
they complain noisily, food is sent. Then they demand
cigarettes, and the officer in charge of the compound
is ordered to supply their regular quota. As if in payment
for goods received, a PW leader passes a note to a guard
at the gate, listing the names of four anti-Communist
hostages they hold. But they refuse to release them, display them (to prove to us they're alive), or say whether
there are any more. Instead, they react by breaking off
the dialogue and holding a noisy mass protest meeting
in the center of the compound.

When the meeting breaks up, a PW detaches himself
from the crowd and delivers another note to the puzzled

51

guards at the gate. This one, in English, says arrogantly, "We will consent to receive Major Evers [an M.P.] in audience at the enclosure gate." The pose of acting the conqueror, rather than the conquered, pays off, for soon Major Evers, unsmiling, shows up on the other side of the gate from a group of grinning PWs. They refuse to parley with him in English (the blind PW interpreter is missing from the group), so we send for my interpreter Mr. Chang, who jabbers at length with the *honcho* and then reports that they will agree to release the four hostages—who they claim are the only ones in the compound who would screen South—if we abandon any further screening attempts. Of course this is something we cannot do.

Still wary, we allow no American personnel in THREE. Late in the afternoon the PWs there call the main hospital building on the compound telephone and ask for U.S. doctors. The orthopedic patients there need changes of dressings and casts. Only a few PWs in THREE show themselves outside their huts, although the weather doesn't seem to bother the other compounds. The wind is still violent but fails to blow away the gray sky, and scattered raindrops continue to fall.

At FOUR, meanwhile, negotiations for screening are working out. "We're ready now," says the compound *honcho* inexplicably. Quickly, tents are set up at the compound gate for fingerprinters, interrogators, and interpreters. FOUR has sixteen hundred medical patients, plus hundreds of PW workers, the majority of whom seem to be clustered along the barbed wire to watch the setting-up of the operation. Six-by-six trucks and two platoons of ambulances begin arriving to receive the screened-North patients (believed in this case to be the smaller number and thus the more practical to transfer out of the compound). They're to go to an empty compound.

The screening runs smoothly, and one by one the ambulances peel off for the new North compound. Strung along the fringe of the plateau by the gate of FOUR, the ambulances overlook the hostile THREE and SIX compounds below as they start off. Trying to incite the North Korean minority in FOUR into making trouble which might complicate the screening nextdoor in FIVE, the Communists in THREE and SIX gather in force along the fence nearest to the road to chant slogans and sing martial songs, all easily heard above on the plateau. The chanting, as loud and impressive in fervor as at a crucial moment in a college football game, succeeds only in frightening more PWs into escaping from THREE and SIX from the opposite side under cover of the demonstration. All are hustled to ELEVEN.

ELEVEN more and more resembles a refugee camp— filled with anti-Communists with dazed expressions on their faces, and few personal effects. Some are even without all their clothing, having fled without chop-bowl, without blankets, often without shoes. Most of the patients who have managed escapes have no medical records or X rays now. So far we have more than four hundred like this in ELEVEN, some of whom are pretty sick.

SIX and THREE are adding to their football-crowd look by waving colorful flags and pennants at the departing screened-North PWs. A sign emblazoned on a blanket fails to take into account the situation in the compound itself: "ALL PW DESIRE TO RETURN HOME." Some of the North Korean, Chinese Communist, and Soviet flags are large handsome ones. "At a distance they don't even look homemade," I say aloud, to nobody in particular.

"Sir," a nearby GI comments, "they've gone one better in SIX: there's a big portrait of Stalin in the Seriously Ill Hut."

Assuming that the security personnel might be interested in the information, I mention the Stalin picture to one of the M.P. officers. His reaction: "So what? I have a picture of Truman in mine." (Harry wouldn't be pleased.)

Little compound SEVEN is rapidly—too rapidly—filling up with PWs who have screened North and have been shuttled down from FOUR. On arrival they all break out previously hidden Communist flags. Some of their leaders begin a conclave even before all potential arrivals are there, and make immediate demands for improved living conditions. What improvements they want, I don't know. It's a bad mistake to hold them where they are now—adjacent to the holdout TWO, where the Communists are busy cheering the arrival nextdoor of each new truckload of comrades. But it's being done in the name of security—grouping North PWs in one area and South PWs in another.

Although the processing continues without serious incident, it rapidly becomes obvious that our loyalty estimate for the compound is embarrassingly off, for 70 per cent want to go North, filling SEVEN to overflowing.

Still the rest of the PWs choosing repatriation are shipped there, and the screening in FOUR is finally completed in the early hours of evening under hastily set up portable floodlights, whose generators chatter like pneumatic drills. In the glare of other floodlights, additional tents are pitched in the small resettled compound—a difficult task in the high winds and deep shadows. The confusion seems overwhelming, but somehow the job gets done. However bungled, the operation is still an important accomplishment, for it marks the first successful screening of *patients,* with the extra complications that go along with mass movement of sick and wounded, the equipment and services necessary to their treatment. Previous screenings had involved only the relatively easy transfer of able-bodied PWs who could walk or ride in trucks.

A memorable incident occurs in FOUR during the screening. Two young brothers—North Korean PWs—part paths in the screening tent, one to go North, the other to stay South, unwilling to return to Communist North Korea. They shake hands American style and go their ways separately.

Opening his mail back at the hut, Lt. Dean (across the potbelly stove from me) tries vainly to hide the fact that one large envelope contained a lacy, brightly colored anniversary card from his wife—their first anniversary. (He's spent all but the first two weeks of that first fifty-two overseas.) Derisive congratulations ring through the hut. "I can remember what my wife *looks* like," says Dean, "but I can't remember what she *feels* like." It reminds me: today is my birthday—number twenty-three. Hardly had a chance to realize it—and cer-

55

tainly won't let anyone else in the hut realize it! I celebrate by relaxing in the sack and reading a paperback copy of the recent Broadway comedy *The Happy Time*.

At night the PWs in THREE, despite chill winds, are seen breaking up the sides of some of their wooden huts. One GI in a passing jeep remarks, bewildered, "They must be crazy, on a night like this, to let in the cold on purpose. What the hell are they trying to prove?" From SIX and THREE, PWs stone the cruising American half-tracks and jeeps, then duck into the darkness behind the first huts near the fences. There is no response from the Americans, who have instructions to take cover if necessary but not to retaliate.

While I'm in the shower hut with Lt. Dean, and the steamy water coming down, the lights go out all over our quarters area. In the darkness Dean spots the glow of the hut's potbelly stove and gingerly lifts the lid. There's enough light to get done.

Back in the darkened hut we lie awake, thinking aloud, until the generator failure is repaired. Someone mentions PW No. 600001, and we all realize that none of us knows what has happened to him, because our concern is with PW patients. No. 600001 can't screen either North or South (I assume), because he's one of the two Japanese prisoners of war I know of. He probably holds some kind of record for PWs. Successively he's been prisoner of the Chinese Communists, Russians, North Koreans, South Koreans, and U.S. For more than eight of the last ten years he's been a PW, this time because he was forced into the Communist Chinese Army (and they call themselves the "Chinese People's Volunteers"!)

from a temporary refuge in Manchuria. Up to now he's been a model prisoner—he's had plenty of practice—while the problem of what to do with him is settled. He's been a PW laborer in one of the hospital workers' compounds, tending the hot-water boilers there. For some reason the Chinese and Korean PWs are awed by him and afraid of him. They leave him alone.

Last month No. 600002 was captured up North—a second Japanese. But he's never come our way.

A bright, sunny, chilly dawn—so cold that we're out of oil for the stove and have to scurry around looking for fuel, which is in short supply. After finding some, we can't find a funnel or other such contrivance to get the oil into the stove. Getting desperate, I take an ax and chop a hole in the top of a steel helmet. Turned upside down, a helmet treated in this fashion makes a pretty good funnel. But it will never be much good as a helmet again.

Hospital and M.P. headquarters are still bending over backward to avoid incidents. They raise hell with Lt. Dean (who is in charge of SEVEN now) because at 0700 he and other officers were eating breakfast before the PWs recently moved to SEVEN had been fed theirs. (I don't believe that all the noise they were making concerned breakfast.) The Communists there are busy demonstrating about something, anyway, and have been since daybreak, waving crudely made North Korean flags (tinted with merthiolate and gentian violet from compound medical stores), loudly singing Red Army songs. An M.P. sound truck pulls up alongside the compound and vainly pleads that they quiet down; but the excuse of not having had the morning meal is too good an opportunity for them to lose, and cries of "American oppressors!" can be heard during the pauses between songs.

Dean, of course, had withheld breakfast from the compound as pressure to stop their demonstrations, but it backfired. Before he can even finish his own breakfast, he's replaced by Capt. John Noonan as compound officer. Although Noonan orders rations sent in immediately, the Communists continue demonstrating—more now, very likely, to celebrate our backing down on the food. They must realize that Dean had been purposely slow about drawing their morning rations when he discovered their undisciplined behavior. But they've prevailed, and he'll be reassigned to some other job within the camp.

The Communists in ONE are observed busily making flags, mutilating medical records, mixing up their own comrades' X rays. Since they've been told by U.S. doctors that medical care depends upon their cooperation, this is a strange kind of defiance—in some cases possibly suicidal. With all this obviously going on inside, there is some question as to whether American medical officers should enter the compound on their rounds (thus condoning the disorder) or whether it is physically safe to do so regardless of moral or medical issues. While a half-dozen doctors, plus a small squad of aid-men, stand by at the sally-port, unable to make up their minds about entering, sixty PWs take advantage of the opportunity to collect at the gate and ask to be let out. All are shipped off by ambulance to FOUR, now a South compound, and as they are loaded, one vehicle at a time, they act joyous and relieved—almost as if they had been set free.

One of the sixty is my oxlike "office boy," Pok, a PW laborer who considers himself (from a wild misunderstanding of what real American office boys do) as fitting the definition of office boy because he helps the PW morgue detail, which operates out of the hospital registrar's office. He was impressed into the North Korean Army when it came down across the thirty-eighth parallel. Given no weapon, only a sack of rice, he was ordered to march ahead of the Communists, along with other reluctant volunteers, probably to absorb the first gunfire. When he consumed all his rations, he deserted.

Wrote home today about the importance of the commitment we've made:

> *It may sound corny, but the 16th and 17th of April were momentous days for men all over the world as a result of the screening begun and accomplished. It signifies a step forward in human history. We dare not turn back. We have committed ourselves irrevocably to a policy unheard of before, the principle that men have the right to ask for our protection from unwanted Communist domination, and that we must guarantee their right to decide for themselves whether they prefer to live under Communism or to reject it. The middle ground of passive looking-on has about disappeared.*

In contrast to events in SEVEN, we are authorized to delay delivery of rations to TWO until the Communists agree to clean up the damage they caused during the night and to destroy the signs they've plastered up reading (in Korean) "GO BACK TO THE U.S." and "KILL THE AMERICANS." We're more lax with ELEVEN, where "freed" anti-Communists wave homemade Republic of Korea and Chinese Nationalist flags. The same thing is going on in TEN, which is now being used as a refugee compound for TB cases. All the South PWs are happy and excited, and think the war is almost over. But almost every PW in TEN has escaped without his medical records.

Negotiations between M.P. officers and Communist *honchos* in SIX are proceeding. Each confrontation becomes a little Panmunjom. Red leaders of course want the screening done on their terms, but are very subtle. They want the Communists to remain in SIX (it's home away from home) and the PWs screened South to go to TEN. They want each PW who escaped their terror to return for his official screening. They want each PW who then decides to stay South to return to his hut to pick up his own hospital charts, clothing, blankets, chop-bowl and chopsticks. It sounds almost reasonable, but any PW naïve enough to do that might either be beaten or killed or be threatened with reprisals to his family, or with a "people's court" trial *in absentia.* Thus acceptance of the proposal would frighten many into deciding to go North after all. The haggling, stalling, and stalking-out is reminiscent of Red diplomacy on every level. Finally, screening is on, but the effect of the "compromise" conditions agreed upon is that patients are intimidated into either leaving all their belongings behind, as they go to the screening tent, or being labeled South by the compound *honchos* before getting to safety.

Screening in SIX proceeds at a limping pace but is completed by dusk. Anti-Communists are shifted to TEN, where medical threatment for all of them is in confusion, for most of them have brought none of their charts and records with them.

While the movement from SIX is going on, the PWs

61

in THREE—on the other side of the dividing fences— are lining up in what seems to be a sort of "regimental parade." More than sixteen hundred of them, some on crutches, some with legs in casts, some walking grimly on wooden "pylons" instead of legs, can be observed organizing themselves into squads, platoons, and companies. Everyone who can get out of bed seems to be in the line of march, and even many of those unable to walk are appearing in the parade in litters borne by PW aid-men. It must be a sign of disloyalty there not to be involved in the demonstration.

The paraders wave Communist flags, banners, and standards and display large paper "floral" wreaths for some reason. Although the whole business seems to be an obvious attempt to intimidate the PWs getting screened in SIX into making the right choice, in appearance it seems a vast funeral procession, with the entire compound participating. Funeral for whom? No bodies are displayed, but the funereal impression is intensified when the PWs stalk slowly around the inside perimeter of the compounds, intoning mournful dirges and then alternating them incongruously with the North Korean Red Army song. The slow pace may be both deliberate and necessary, for the lame and the halt and the litter-borne move along the parade path with difficulty, dragging themselves on, no doubt, by the strength of their fanaticism and their hate.

The procession continues without interruption from 1100 to 1300, an impressive and awesome spectacle, as seen from inside SIX and then from the plateau above

THREE. It seems like a dream (nightmare variety) seen from a great distance.

All afternoon THREE remains quiet, but at night the PWs build a big bonfire. We don't know what's being burned, but hopefully guess that a good deal of their parade decorations are being destroyed so that we won't seize them, and so we won't feel that their presence in the compound should deny the PWs medical care when they decide they want it.

In the Women's Compound the Communists spend the afternoon trying to break down the barbed wire separating them from the screened-South women. There is the usual screaming, singing, flag-waving, rock-throwing— and some casualties on both sides—before the women quiet down, and doctors feel that it's safe to check inside.

It's quiet enough while the breaks and bruises are dressed, but trouble breaks out again immediately afterward and continues sporadically through the night. One female is injured twice—in each demonstration. While splinting this tangle-haired innocent's hand, Lt. Jenks asks her how she injured it. "It broke all of a sudden," she says.

These women are a strange crew. Some of the female prisoners claim to have been doctors and nurses, but some of the "nurses" seem to have followed an older profession of service to armies. Many are as surly and fanatical as the men, and can be believed when they claim to have borne arms as well as children. Several have small children with them, and more have been born here in captivity. (Are children born to PWs also PWs?)

Oblivious to the sound and the fury, and unaware of

ideology, the PW tots play in the dirt with stones, empty tin cans, and bits of wood and cloth. Oblivious, too, to the fact that, officially, many of them don't exist. Late in January the fingerprinting and identification teams which were methodically preparing for the screening operation (until they met with mass resistance from PWs on Koje) were working here, and discovered eighteen infants (born in captivity) belonging to women PWs whom we counted technically as patients in order to get the children cared for. And none of the infants was counted in our "head count" of PWs, for only prisoners of war can be treated at this hospital, and I would have had to have them classified—newborn—as PWs. The way I've been getting around it is—on paper but not in fact—to ignore their existence. The idea horrifies some quarters in officialdom, now that they know about it. Under the slave system in the South, a child born to a slave was a slave also—by accident of birth. I pointed this out at the time, drawing the parallel vigorously and insisting that we would be labeling a newborn infant as a Communist prisoner of war for a similar misfortune of birth. It was very much overstated and melodramatic, and the reaction I got was thorough bewilderment. So the babies don't exist and haven't been fingerprinted, I assume. They won't have to begin their lives with a "prison record" and no one knows whether they should be screened when they grow up—they'll have enough trouble later, just trying to grow up, whether their mothers go North or South.

Radiantly joyous now, the South Koreans in FOUR continue to release their pent-up tension. They salute

U.S. soldiers smartly and walk about with a jaunty air, belying the fact that most of them are patients. Their features seem frozen into permanent smiles.

There's interesting news from Koje, our southern, and more active, front. The screening there is reported now to be as complete as it can get without further bloodshed. Eighty-five thousand Communist PWs—a good many of them fanatical—remain there after "Operation Spread-out" (the movement of screened-South PWs to mainland camps) comes to a temporary halt. It's a wait-and-see game on a larger scale than ours, for American screening teams there have been refused entrance to the remaining compounds, which are holding out with some unknown hope in mind. All the screened Koreans who have chosen to stay South so far are in five mainland camps, while the Chinese who elected to "forcibly resist repatriation" have been moved to Cheju Island, far south of Koje.

I got four birthday cards today.

A gray, cloudy day. With the morning quiet, the hospital is operating on a limping sort of routine in the open compounds. The only screening is the processing of anti-Communist refugees in TEN and ELEVEN. The PW women are still recuperating; many have severe laryngitis due to their vocal enthusiasm, for they refuse to quiet down until their throats give way.

Morale is so high in FOUR that it lifts our own. Pok is all smiles and salutes me as I walk in. We let the PWs in FOUR make ROK flags to work off their enthusiasm, but have supplied no materials. Still, they get them. Directing their enthusiasm into other channels, they also try to heave rocks down into SIX, but the distance is too great. They only endanger our patrols.

On an "invitation" from the PWs via a note handed through the fence to Capt. Sands, the chief compound doctor, medical officers and GIs move back into THREE. The *honcho* shows the captain and his sergeant that much of the damage has been cleared away (probably in the bonfires they've been having). But, insists the *honcho*, they want dressings, not screening. Just about the same thing is happening in ONE, where the dissidents offer apologies for past misbehavior. There the PW monitor for hut ⹂8 asks the American medical officer (following his apology), "Now we can have our dressings changed and more medication—yes?" Meanwhile more PWs take advantage of the opportunity to leave ONE safely. When they ask to leave—and are promptly let out —the Communists in ONE begin inciting trouble again, and medical personnel evacuate even before they are able to finish their first rounds.

At 1300 hours, the Communists in THREE begin to hold political meetings, and the Americans sigh wearily to each other and walk out again (they had been promised no more meetings or demonstrations while our personnel were in the compound). The meetings coincide with a choral interlude from compound companions TWO and SEVEN, who accompany the North Korean Red Army songs with vigorous waving of homemade flags. After a warning, SEVEN grows quiet and puts the bunting away, but TWO refuses to lower its flags from huts and tents. Then the ROK colonel in charge of the tower guards serves an ultimatum—his patience at an end —that he will send in his Korean troops to do the job if the flags are not down within ten minutes. Eight minutes later, by my PX watch, the flags come down. (Later we learn that he has been warned not to threaten force again, as orders to use force have to come from very high up, and we'd be in the embarrassing position of not being able to make good on our threats. As if what's going on now isn't embarrassing!)

Although they've backed down, there's a sense of uneasiness in the camp that the PWs know that the ROK bluster was all bluff. Although they remain quiet, the *honchos* in TWO post their own club-wielding guards along the interior perimeter, as if to dare the ROK commandant. Drizzle, fog, and darkness settle early over the area, and we drift to our huts to wait it out.

67

Incident in FOUR as told to me over a can of beer by the compound officer, Lt. Thomas: Chinese PW in SIX fears for his life as he refuses to avow any political sympathies (although he had screened North). He flees to the compound admissions hut at the sally-port and pleads with the GI on duty to transfer him to another compound. On the assumption that he actually is anti-Communist, but naïvely thought at first that it would be safe to go home, he is shipped to FOUR (which the PW does not know is entirely screened-South), and brought to the Chinese *honcho* for the compound.

The *honcho* interrogates the frightened expatriate: "Are you Communist?"

(no answer)

"Are you anti-Communist?"

(no answer)

The Chinese *honcho,* ripping open his shirt to show his Nationalist tattoo: "Well, I'm an anti-Communist!"

The new arrival bares his chest, exposing an identical tattoo. Nothing more is spoken. Each rushes forward to embrace the other.

Cold, steady rain falling. It's Sunday but looks like the other six days each week. First item of business proves to be Wang Yin Soo, the PW who screened North but is now in a South compound. The red tape to explain his being rescreened, or unscreened, will probably turn out to be enormous; and when the news of it reaches Panmunjom it will no doubt cause at least one vituperative speech and the cancellation of at least one session of the truce talks.

The PWs in THREE call M.P. headquarters on the compound telephone to announce brazenly that if regular medical treatment isn't forthcoming, they'll break into the compound supply hut and let the PW doctors take care of treatment from now on. These PW physicians are a puzzle. Resident in each compound, they live with their troops in the same way they did before capture. In some cases their loyalty to Communism is obvious and vocal, and as intellectuals of a sort they assume a place in the leadership vacuum. Most of them seem as little committed to Communism as they are to medicine, and it's a rare one whose training as a doctor seems adequate. A few seem to be giving us a line to swallow, and perhaps were never doctors at all—perhaps rather pharmacists or male nurses or something allied to the profession, which supplies them with a basic knowledge on which to build. But we need all the PW doctors we can get, so we can't be too suspicious. The same with

PW "nurses"—many of them seem to have become interested in nursing on being captured.

Treatment is "on" again in ONE, but the Reds are warned that further display of flags or of red stars (they wore them on their clothes and posted them in their huts yesterday) will mean no more visits from American doctors. Only SIX (of the North compounds) is fully cooperative, and medical treatment is restored there.

TWO is off on a flag-waving, singing binge again. Even some PWs supposed to be seriously ill are recognized by our doctors as being in the line of march. Also some supposed psycho cases. SEVEN (nextdoor) is unruly too, which puts the hospital Admissions and Dispositions office, located in the forward area between SEVEN and TWO, in an untenable position, like living in a compound sally-port. And now and then rocks bounce in, especially once twilight comes. My men there are willing to stay to receive new arrivals, but point out that they don't feel very secure after dark any more, and this puts a strain upon their concentration during all-night pinochle games. Thinking of the dangers of a night breakthrough, or even more limited violence upon men surrounded on three sides by hostile PWs, I make up my mind to evacuate the area. The permission is easily granted, and we use our ambulances to move admission records and other movable equipment to the main hospital building, taking over the dim, rickety, unused lobby. From my Registrar's office on the second floor I look out on what must be the weirdest such job going: we have no idea how many patients we now have, or who they are, or what's wrong with them; we have no idea how many have died, been murdered, escaped, switched records or identities, or otherwise disappeared into oblivion. But at the end of the month we'll have to fill out the usual pile of official forms (meant for small, clean, quiet post hospitals) as if we do know.

The PWs now run freely back and forth in the former Admissions and Dispositions area, including the Quonset hut. To punish TWO, hospital headquarters orders rations cut off for the compound until order is restored, but the directive is countermanded by M.P. headquarters. After the food arrives, the singing and marching begin again in TWO, but a sudden rainstorm makes the show brief, and no more flags are seen all day except for a taunting South Korean flag high up in FOUR. When the rains taper off, THREE messages to have medics back again, and promises good behavior (again) if we don't try any overt or subtle screening. Apprehensive that innocent anti-Communist prisoners would suffer, the C.O. continues the indefinite postponement. But this can't go on forever.

I'm Officer of the Day—which really means the night. There's been pressure on us during the emergency to wear weapons at all times (except inside a prison compound). Officers are to carry a .45 or at least sling a carbine over one's shoulder; but even on O.D. duty—even while presiding at the traditional guard mount—I decline to buckle on the O.D.'s .45, claiming that, considering my demonstrable inefficiency with firearms, it was in the best interests of the United States Army to permit me the idiosyncrasy.

On duty (to pass the time) I listen to the PWs as

they use the camp phone system to jabber to other PWs in compounds out of voice (or stone with message attached) range. Too bad my smattering of Chinese, Japanese, and Korean isn't better. But headquarters up the hill has the connection to all phones and condones the chatter because S-2 is monitoring the calls. One PW in THREE even calls up the Medical Officer of the Day, Capt. Reede, and gets some professional advice, given grudgingly. "At home," he tells me, "I don't prescribe over the phone for anybody, not even friends. And here I do it for someone who would kill me if he could!"

At midnight the situation is the way an O.D. likes it —cold, clear, and quiet. But the telephone lines are still eerie.

The M.O.D. and I are up early, awakened by a well-organized sunrise ceremony in ONE, right nearby. Large North Korean, Chinese Communist, and Russian flags are displayed. Obviously there are over a thousand in the chorus, many battle casualties among them, some wearing little more than bandages, casts, and crutches. One PW with no legs stands on his stumps waving a flag. The ceremony ends very abruptly, and the participants disperse, just before 0800—the time American medics usually (if safe) arrive at the compound for rounds. By the time they arrive, ONE is as peaceful and routine as if nothing had happened.

Just in time to miss the spectacle is the area commanding general, who shows up at the camp command post with little advance notice. "Had I known he was coming," Sgt. Klinghoffer tells me, "I would have had the boys in ONE keep the floor show going a little longer." I console him with the thought that there will be another opportunity.

The General claims—we've heard it before—that negotiations are at a delicate stage and that we mustn't provoke a break in the truce talks by blundering into violence here. Much is made of the possible propaganda value to the enemy of our intimidating hospital patients. Screening, we're told, is not an excuse for violence by us: force is to be employed only when necessary to prevent escapes.

A strange situation prevails in FIVE. The anti-Communist *honcho* has the situation literally in hand. His monitors (with menacing cot-end clubs and barbed-wire flails) patrol the area and keep the 75 per cent Red compound under control. With this help the screening goes smoothly: those choosing to stay South go quietly to TEN; the others remain, some with a biding-their-time glare in their eyes. One seriously ill patient expires as he is carried in on a litter to be screened. A laconic and death-hardened GI ambulance driver, cheated of a passenger, observes, "I wonder if he chose heaven or hell."

ONE, TWO, THREE, and SEVEN are all closed again by afternoon, the excuse being that each presents a real danger to our personnel. Very likely true, but more to the point is that each still have PW hostages. SIX is in operation again, with the Reds sheepishly kowtowing. Across from FIVE, the screened-North females hold a drill, taking seriously the business of inciting the Communists in FIVE to resist screening; but it proceeds without incident. The women keep marching and singing all morning and afternoon—a disconcerting sight from a distance because they've all been issued WAC overcoats.

With FIVE apparently pacified easily, it's decided to search the long hut believed to be the center of resistance agitation in the compound, now that all the anti-Communists have been evacuated. A shakedown team of military police handles the job, and I send a few of my men to check identities at the same time, for we now have more medical records than PWs for the compound. The stripping and searching of PWs, and PW huts and

tents, usually results in the discovery of amazing quanti-
ties of contraband somehow sneaked into, or manufac-
tured within, the compounds: crude weapons, *sake*,
money, dried fish, squid and octopi, printed or hand-
copied Communist propaganda tracts, PX wristwatches,
the now-inevitable Red flags, extra clothes stolen from
the sick or the dead, drugs (the most valuable bartering
item), and so on. Usually the operation is routine—or
at least it was routine until the screening rebellion.

The surprise to me here is not the spectacle of thirty-
seven patients all standing nude in their hut while M.P.s
go through their clothes, pulling out a dried octopus
here and 1000-Won notes there—the curious thing about
the procedure is that each completely naked PW holds
a Bible (English-Korean) in his hand. An M.P. officer
explains to me that many PWs in the compound had
been converted before the screening troubles began, and
that the odd sight of thirty-seven naked communist PWs,
each holding a Bible, is due to the M.P. ruling that PWs
are allowed to keep their Bibles.

As he tells me about the baffling religious revival, and
I pontificate that perhaps the reason is the Communists'
desire to learn the very useful English language, a prisoner accidentally drops his copy of the Scriptures. As it
hits the floor, 1000-Won notes catapult out from between its pages. The embarassed PW scoops up the
money—a formidable bankroll—but, having no clothes on,
has no place to conceal it. Our scrutiny shifts to the
bulky Bibles, and the M.P.s scan them all with no religious
end in mind; reducing each PW to poverty. When the
Bibles—now purified—are offered back, some of the PWs

stonily refuse to accept them. These, and the confiscated material collected, are loaded into an empty truck, and the prisoners are left with a PW doctor to supervise the reassembly of their clothing.

A hospital annex is now under construction several miles away. It's to house all our screened-South patients, so civil war won't continue after the job of separating Communists from anti-Communists is completed. I haven't been out to see the site chosen, but the comments from officers who went out with the first GI and PW work crews aren't very favorable. One comment: "They could have picked a location a *little* closer—as long as it was out of sight of the Communist compounds." One GI, asked what kind of progress has been made on the annex in the first day's work: "Well you'd be amazed, yesterday it was just a rice paddy. And today it's still just a rice paddy." But the job will be rushed to completion, with all the labor and security personnel that can be spared.

Saw a movie (part of it, anyway) in our outdoor "Paddy Theater": an *Arabian Nights* type of film whose title I don't know, as the first part was missing. It probably ended the way most of this species end, but I'm not sure of that either, as not only was the beginning missing but the end as well. The fragment went over well with the GIs, though, providing endless opportunities for speculation; and all the recently arrived men are getting buttonholed to find out if the movie resembles anything seen in the States lately. "Man," says one teen-aged recruit, "my dad could answer that better: it looked like it was from his time, if they had Technicolor in those days." One attraction of the movie: the sound track drowns out the PW shrieking and chanting for a while.

To make up for the missing segments of film, I guess, we also are treated to a short feature, also in glorious Technicolor, called *This Is Korea*. Now we know what the Marines are doing.

Another sunny, clear, chill day. Screening teams show up again at the gate of TWO—hopefully—but are told firmly by the compound commissars that they are "not ready." The team departs, with its equipment. Soon, in response to the "provocation," a PW elite squad of fifty Koreans (patients?) marches in tight formation to the front gate of the compound and halts. All (in unison) give Soviet-style clenched-fist salutes while a *honcho* conducts them in cheers in English ("Death to Americans! . . . Down with American Imperialists!") and in North Korean and Russian songs. After a last upraising of arms in the clenched-fist salute, they about-face and depart, marching back briskly into the interior of the compound.

There is no such atmosphere of seriousness in SIX's belligerence. There the Communists are busy showing—dramatically—how sure they are of themselves by staging a foot race on the hard-packed earth of the long main compound street, with representatives of each ward participating and a master of ceremonies leading off the program with a series of Communist cheers. A large audience inside the compound and out (including PWs high up above them in FOUR) watches in a shimmering sun that somehow fails to warm. The lean, limber winner—by a great margin, and not even breathing hard at the finish—turns out to be a patient recorded as having a serious lung ailment. According to his X rays he should not even have been able to get off his back.

We investigate rapidly—since the compound still appears to be safe—and discover that he arrived here with apparently stolen X rays and papers just before the big trouble began. It is not even necessary to take a corroborative X ray.

An expression of chagrin alters his winner's smile when we mark his papers for immediate discharge (and Kojedo). Immediately on realizing what is happening to him, he regains composure and tells us confidently, "I will be back." If he makes it again, we'll know—but not immediately—for whatever new name and medical records he adopts as his own next time will have to be checked against *his* fingerprints. By that time he may have already used the hospital as his message center—so we understand his cockiness and, with a sense of helplessness, pack him on a truck.

Near the barbed wire his comrades stand silently, watching. Then, as the truck moves off, they move toward their common boundary with THREE to watch the military preparations underway inside.

The PWs in ONE are again strutting about with homemade red stars on their caps (U. S. Army fatigue caps), which they've stiffened inside with cardboard to resemble the Communist type of military hat. And they're refusing to allow the gate to be opened except to let food in. Wary of attempts to remove their insignia, each time they see the possibility of the gate being opened or forced, they send a human barricade against it, several PWs deep.

In THREE the PWs have constructed a more permanent barricade by piling refuse before their main gate, and the activity stirs them into more colorful defiance. Red flags with a yellow star in the upper corner near the staff, surrounded by a half circle of smaller yellow stars, go up on all tents and huts—the Red Chinese standard. With the flag raising comes more of the clenched-fist saluting and slogan chanting. It's getting monotonous now, and even the PWs know it, for the noise fizzles out at about noon.

FIVE is now a model Communist compound, quiet and orderly, as the medical officer in charge, Capt. Fleming, manages to keep them in line. Although he must be the youngest doctor we have, the PWs have great respect for his firmness. Patients he finds agitating trouble suddenly are diagnosed as having miraculously recovered, and pronounced fit for discharge.

Not much business these days for "Digger" and his crew, for neither Koje nor the line is sending us many casualties. Koje is retaining theirs so far for security reasons and the line has only been active sporadically. Sitting nearby and killing time by gradually darkening a piece of paper with straight, parallel pencil lines, Digger looks up and asks me: "Sir, do you think I could get a temporary transfer to Koje-do? I'd be more useful there."

He's been reading the casualty reports I've been getting from the growing little hospital on the island. I tell him that I would recommend he be given a psychiatric examination if he applied for a transfer there. But, like the surgeons, he's itching to practice his profession, and the closest he can get to it here, while serving out his draft time, is as corporal of my morgue detail, for in

80

civilian life he was an undertaker. Here his hearse is a six-by-six truck with trailer attached.

"You know," he mulls aloud, "in a way the work is harder here because the names of the PWs are all so alike. I can't really remember one case from another by matching it to a name, like I used to do back home. Why, I can tell you the special problems—if there were any—involved in any case I ever embalmed.

"What I really used to like was when customers used to come to our establishment to shop in advance—you know, to pick out the casket in which they thought they'd look best.

"And d'ya know—they were often wrong!"

We hear at a hospital staff session that GHQ has been asked for authority to cut off the food supply from any compound resisting screening (or, euphemistically, the transfer of patients from one ward to another, in the interests of more efficient medical care). The aim is to coerce ONE, TWO, and THREE, the only holdouts now.

Capt. Valentine, a camp security officer, tells me more details of the plan, and its alternatives, as we patrol the outer perimeter at night—the narrow dirt road skirting the compounds and the rice paddies. One idea is that the PWs won't be denied food but will have to leave their wards and go out their gate to get it, rather than have it brought inside. In this way any PW who wanted to go South could escape intimidation merely by going to get his chop-bowl filled. By refusing to return to his compound he would, in effect, be screening South.

It seems to me an attempt to escape responsibility. My only comment to Valentine is that the plan doesn't

81

solve the problem of giving bedridden patients an opportunity to choose whether or not they wanted to go back home. And that neither would it get them fed.

As we jeep along, the tangled barbed wire and squat ROK guard towers twist the moonlight into strange shadows. The Korean tower sentries now stand silently in the cool air, now thump their boots on the wooden platforms to keep warm—their syncopated drum taps are the only sounds in the night to compete with the droning vehicle motors. We pass tanks and jeeps on the slow pace of regular patrol, half-tracks with 50-caliber machine guns perched on rocky prominences, pointing their "quad-fifties" toward the quiet hospital.

The silence is deceptive, for it doesn't connote inactivity. The PWs in TWO have their own guards pacing back and forth below the ROK sentries. In THREE, PWs don't even look up as we go by in the jeep: they're too busy making knives and spears from aluminum litter poles. In SIX, squads are marching in the near-darkness, remote from the lights thrown on the outer edges of the compound. It appears as if they consider themselves the guardians of holdout THREE, because of the common fence and gate; and when they march along the fence they share with THREE, their gait turns into a strut. Even in ONE, alone in a corner of the camp, there is also marching and drilling going on. Yet it still seems oppressively quiet.

Half-tracks with 50-caliber machine guns perched on rocky prominences, pointing their "quad-fifties" toward the quiet hospital.

On the ruse of shifting them to equally Red FIVE, twenty-five fanatics and troublemakers are spirited out of SIX and shipped directly to Koje. Included is old, dying, wispy bearded "Commissar," who plots from his deathbed and is living proof of the tenacity of one's will to live. He says he's sixty-two—very old for a Korean—but he looks much older. For all we know he is a high-ranking officer, but almost every PW admits only to being a private: a handy Communist technique to prevent our identifying and segregating their leaders. It sometimes works—and provides them with high-level leadership— until we notice some unusual deference being paid to a "private."

The rations-withholding request is back in our laps again, and the camp brass has had a meeting with the area general to plan the next move. Withholding of food is not ruled out as an extreme measure, but it is temporarily disallowed on the premise that it is certain to cause riots. The decision instead is to suspend all but emergency medical care for ONE, TWO, and THREE, since their undisciplined state prevents regular medical care and raises questions of physical safety for our medical personnel. "Gate clinics" (euphemism courtesy of hospital C.O.) are to be set up in tents near the main gate of each holdout compound for treatment of sick prisoners who come or who are carried by PW aid-men to the gate of the sally-port.

Reports that PWs in the holdout compounds are again breaking up some of their wooden huts—they're really three standard huts placed end to end, to accommodate about a hundred patients in all—lead to renewed speculation about the reasons. Security officers think that the PWs are just making more rubble for barricade purposes —in case we try to force entry. A few more imaginative souls think that the PWs may be making wooden ladders (doing the carpentry inside their huts) in preparation for a breakout. A doctor who has been here a long time thinks that the Communists are just bent on destroying property, to make as much trouble for us as they can. But that doesn't explain their doing the breakup work only after dark.

I hear of a further worry based upon increasing guerrilla activity in the vicinity of the enclosure (a half-track was attacked yesterday)—that an attempt from without might be made to release the PWs. They could then take to the hills. It seems unbelieveable that thousands of patients might jeopardize their lives this way.

Cold and overcast. SIX is almost out of control because of the departure of the obnoxious twenty-five. Like weeds, new agitators seem to spring up as soon as the old ones are out of the way. The angry mob blames PW Dr. Chung for abetting "Commissar's" exit to Koje, while he disclaims any collusion, and threatens to commit suicide to save his honor. While the uproar continues, the GIs prudently evacuate the compound, returning later to find Dr. Chung morosely on the job.

The aid-station "clinics" feebly continue our efforts to act like a hospital. Less than a dozen patients have been treated at the three of them today. *Honchos* are reluctant to let PWs of dubious political allegiance through the gate for treatment. PW militia in the closed compounds drill and strut in outlandish "uniforms" made from PW-issue clothing. Some unexplainably have swastika emblems as shoulder patches. We do doubletakes each time we spot one.

One of our chief men in internal medicine has become fed up with sitting on his hands and with having so many Korean doctors who assist the American medical staff join us in doing nothing. Today he decided to hold a brush-up-on-your-medicine session for the Koreans, whose clinical background at best is shaky. They filled the X-ray hut to hear him discuss problem TB cases —whether they should be continued on antibiotics, recommended for surgery when conditions return to "normal," or discharged to stockade. He held up various X rays to the light so that all the Korean doctors could see them. Each time an apparently negative chest plate was displayed, he could hear a faint, singing sound from the back row of the group. The next time he pulled out an X ray belonging to a patient slated for discharge, he cocked his ear for suspicious sounds from the rear.

Sure enough, soon, to the melody of the *Hallelujah!* repetitions in Handel's *Hallelujah Chorus,* he heard the words singsonged, '*Sayonára—sayonára—sayonára . . .* '"

He pounced on the physician-chorus and asked them where they picked up this method of announcing the eligibility of a patient for discharge; and he got the answer, "That's what Capt. Fleming sing each time he find a negative X ray."

Now that the story is out, the hut rings tonight with the pseudo-Handelian "*Sayonara* Chorus," but it will probably be forgotten by tomorrow—or as soon as everyone is sober.

Our private little cold war continues in the miserable rain and overcast. Women make the most noise, as usual. SIX is still in turmoil: we evacuate, return, evacuate. In the closed compounds *honchos* let a few patients out to the "gate clinics": four from ONE, one from TWO, none from THREE.

Even mail delivery lags. All that comes for me today is a picture postcard from a vacationing friend, with a Miami Beach scene described on the back: *An express highway for the motorist parallels a flower and palm lined yacht canal between Lake Pancoast and Biscayne Bay.* The note:

> *"Dear Stan,*
> *It is with slightly awkward feelings that I write this card, realizing the differences in our present locales. Sure hope that by the time this card arrives you will be all set for departure to the States."*

Looking for a place to display the card, I see my ax-punctured helmet, hanging by its chin strap from a nail in the wall behind my sack. The inside webbing of the helmet liner is a good place to keep letters.

Lt. Knox is—in the drizzle—planting mint outside his hut. He says that he needs something to remind him of South Carolina and keep his morale up—and that visions of future mint juleps are the answer. He's made a little picket fence of tongue-depressors around his planting, and optimistically predicts that in Korea's richly fecal soil his mint will prosper.

A guerrilla raid over the hill is reported; sentries shot and weapons stolen.

The PW spokesmen in ONE reiterate that they "will die before permitting illegal screening." TWO decides to refuse all gate-clinic care as being an insult to their status as patients and a violation of the Geneva treaties governing PW care (which the Communists never signed and don't adhere to). THREE produces the day's most amazing gesture of defiance: a group of orthopedic patients rip off their casts and throw the debris onto the refuse pile blocking the main compound gate. (Perhaps the PW medics inside will quietly replace them somehow— now that they've "shown us" what they think of our medical treatment. There are medical supply huts in each compound that the PWs can break into for basic supplies like gauze and plaster.) At least SIX is quiet again, apparently realizing that the "Commissar" is already over the water to Koje, where he can dream of operations on a larger scale.

Late at night comes word that the guerrillas showed up again at the ROK ammo dump over the hill, and in another attack shot up an American staff car killing a lieutenant colonel and his driver. Now no one is to be permitted to leave the camp enclosure after dark for other than duty reasons. To some this will come as a great personal sacrifice—and the economy of some of the local villages may suffer. They're the GIs' source of illegal alcohol, exotic foods (hard on the intestines but at least a change of diet), and sex. Very likely too, they're the source of security leaks to the Communists and illegal trade with the prisoners. Perhaps the blanket shortage will end now, for a while.

Though there isn't much to do, and more and more doctors spend a good part of each day—and evening— in their huts, there is a conspicuous falling off in conversation. And a conspicuous increase in reading (anything), letter writing, and drinking. It seems that the less there is to write about, the longer the letters get. I'm beginning to run out of things to write home, and have started to use wider margins and more space between the lines, so that the letter looks like the usual size, although it doesn't say anything.

Lt. Herman, looking up from his letter writing, comments to no one in particular, "This can't go on forever!" No one answers him. Still, we know that something has got to give, because the status quo we've settled into uncomfortably can't be any more permanent than a sit-down strike or a hunger strike. A strike by patients in a hospital against medical care is like a strike by camels in a desert against water.

Five PWs escape before dawn from FOUR; only one recaptured. They bribed a ROK guard (of course PWs aren't supposed to have any money, but have all kinds of ways to get it anyway). I wouldn't want to be that guard, now that the evidence has returned.

Another PW is captured trying to go over the fence —in bright sunlight. He wouldn't say why.

A lot of new battle casualties arriving today: this war doesn't seem to respect Sunday as a day of rest. Each newly captured prisoner is now screened—if he's in condition for it—as soon as he's admitted to the hospital. It's surprising that most new casualties want to stay South, particularly the Chinese. It seems that the most fanatical Communists are the ones who have spent long months brooding over their wounds while behind barbed wire. The casualties fresh from the line don't want to go back North: they remember it too clearly.

There's been lots of lusty singing from the holdout compounds, but no reported violence today. I must be getting jaded: the North Korean Red Army song is beginning to sound a lot like "Anchors Aweigh." The PWs in SEVEN have a new way to rub in their delight at the mess we're in. They let TWO, on the other side of the fence, do most of the singing and chanting, while they strut about with flags and insignia, have regular interior sentry posts and complete military discipline—and (with arrogant leering) salute each American officer who passes by. And every medical officer, at least, has to, because it's on the way to the hospital officer's huts. It's a very uncomfortable feeling.

Our gate clinics might as well be closed. The *honchos* won't permit the desperately sick or wounded to be carried there on litters, and all the other patients not sufficiently fanatical to refuse treatment on principle are too intimidated. At ONE the only business at the sallyport is the delivery of a letter, intended for the C.O., to the attending doctor at the gate clinic. It seems to have no connection with the realities of the situation:

> *We who are in this ward feel that there is not enough medicine being done. We want to state the following:*
>
> *1. Most of us who have been operated on have suffered greatly from drainage from wounds, and when the weather is cold, the pain and drainage come back. So if you would supply enough medicine and nourishment for us inside for our PW doctors we will much appreciate it.*
>
> *2. The reason we refuse your surgery is that you are careless in your operations. Sometimes you cut when you need not cut and sometimes you kill those who need not be killed.*
>
> *3. In the nighttime you leave the surgical technique, and practice only in the daytime. In this way, too, you are murdering us.*
>
> *4. When patients are in your hands, American soldiers hit us and scare us. Particularly that fat soldier in post-op hits us at random. [South Korean] Aid-boys treat us the same way. When you*

do not get rid of our pains and allow us to be hit, you are killing us.

Please consider these points concerning why we cannot accept the kind of medical care you give us. They concern the dignity of your country. What kind of honorable things can you carry out in the future unless you stop the mistreating and killing of invalids?

All Patients in Compound One

We read the message as saying, aside from minor gripes and form-letter denunciations, that the Communists want us to let their PW doctors have all the supplies they need inside so that they can go on holding out. Any other treatment we offer is—by this reasoning—malpractice. Whether the diatribe against the post-op ward (and the "fat soldier") has any substance, I don't know, but it sounds more like the Communists' fear that if we remove a patient from the compound sally-port to post-op for further treatment, they've lost control of him and his screening choice.

Capt. Hank Lesser tells me that he had to do mass anesthetizing when the new casualties from the line were rolling in earlier in the day. He would stand at the entrance to the operating rooms area and as a PW was led or carried in, he'd punch his hypo into the proper places, depending on the nature of the wound. In the confusion, one slipped by him—as he discovered when Col. McKissick (the new chief of surgery) started to poke his scalpel into the bayonet wound in the buttock of one PW. The Chinese jumped off the table and hobbled away as fast as he could, screaming to Hank what

95

in Chinese was obviously equivalent to "Hurry, damn it, put the fire out!" Another patient in the group had his arm anesthetized via nerve block so that a bullet could be removed from it. When all feeling left his arm, he began to scream in a torrent of Chinese that his arm was cut off, and no amount of convincing could reassure him until his arm was freed again and he could see for himself that it was still firmly attached.

Among the new battle casualties are a group of Chinese—a captain, a corporal, and three privates—who were a puzzle at first, for, although they've just been taken prisoner, all have festering wounds which appear to be a month old or more. It appears—on interrogation—that all of them were wounded some time ago but were unable to get medical treatment when they returned to their unit. Either their wounds weren't considered severe enough or else they were shunted away because of a flood of more serious casualties. Anyway, they were returned to duty, smarting from the increasingly painful retained metal fragments. When that happened, the captain and his squad began figuring out a way to get the metal extracted from their arms, legs, backs, and especially from what they sat on. The rest was easy. They courageously volunteered to go out on a dangerous patrol, the object of their reconnaissance an American-held hill, behind which they knew was the battalion aid station of a U.S. regiment. When they got close enough to be spotted, they saw to it that they were captured: a sort of inverted success story.

Toward evening, disturbances begin again in Women's Compound, on the strength of a rumor that all female

PWs are going to be shipped to Koje imminently. I haven't heard of such an order, but PW information is usually reliable. Their screaming and rock throwing goes on into the night—a self-perpetuating situation, for as long as their aim is good, they never need run out of rocks to heave at each other.

A convoy of trucks arrives to convey all the PW women screened North (more than six hundred) to a debarkation point for Koje-do. Sullenly, and as uncooperatively as possible, hands jammed into overcoat pockets, they permit themselves to be herded into the vehicles. Then, as the convoy gets going, they unleash a parting flurry of rocks, heaving them amid lusty screaming while their long black hair blows about their faces in gale-driven rain. The rain gathers force, driving curious PWs in nearby compounds away from the fences and into their nuts and tents, effectively dampening any sympathetic outbreak.

Few discharges of patients in the rain and mud. But came upon one of the more unusual ones when an already screened-South North Korean captain was delivered to us for release by Lt. Jenks. Patients often try to hide from the American medical officer when he's making ward rounds, for fear of being discharged to duty status—which could mean a work detail. This "patient" is one of the most successful at the game that I've discovered so far: he's been evading American doctors since last September, has spent the winter here, and any medical records he possessed when he was first admitted have long since disappeared. He may even have been legitimately sick or wounded when he first arrived, but probably did so under another name, and may even be calling himself a captain now because under international law an officer PW isn't supposed to be put on forced labor. In order to get rid of him, he had to be made acceptable for discharge, which meant (in part) concocting a medical chart with a dischargeable reason on it. It could merely have said "malingerer," but Jenks's diagnosis is "Seven months' rest???"

Holding the unfolded, otherwise empty narrow blue chart in front of me, one of my GIs asks, "What do I do with this one, sir?"

I tell him to let his imagination run wild and devise something interesting—but medical.

Drearily the rain continues into the quiet night. Mud and calm. Slippery, slimy calm.

A movie is being shown at the GI mess hall, and another in the officers' mess, but some of us never even check to see what they are. Instead, we base an evening's entertainment on cheese, crackers, and some onions lifted from a newly arrived shipment. Never ate such powerful onions: we cried as we sliced them, cried as we salted them, cried as we ate them, and with tears streaming down our faces agreed that they were great.

The aroma in the hut is so pungent that it brings tears to the eyes of residents returning from the movie. Some complain that the mud and rain are preferable to the atmosphere inside. Then they come in and complain.

It can't be nearly so bad as last week, when Lt. Dean got a package from home—limburger cheese. Even I left, then.

Cloudy, cold, dreary. Just the right kind of morning for us to find a hanging in the compounds (FOUR this time) at dawn. It looks like a suicide, but that doesn't mean it is.

In the early morning hours the first units of the —th Infantry Regiment arrive from the front to augment security here. They have full and reassuring equipment. Moving into an empty PW compound to set up their camp, one infantryman calls out to us the old joke (it always works): "This is the worst part of Texas I've ever been in!" Hope they like it here.

More than ever we're on the alert for a guerrilla link-up but can't imagine where there'd be sufficient local (outside) strength for it.

The hospital C.O. rushes in to see me to get data on PWs in the closed compounds for a conference with the area general today. Since up-to-date information is impossible to get, we use our imaginations, plus what we know of escapees and deaths, and project some figures. The reason for the hurry is that UN negotiators are supposed to present their latest package proposal at Panmunjom today.

Everybody is irritable and jumpy because of the approach of May Day, a traditional time for Communist fireworks. But the only sign of PW activity is close-order drill in THREE at night, while the —th Regiment sends patrols into the hills around us to probe for possible trouble from the outside.

The area general arrives at the camp command post before 0800. This time he's in time to hear the compounds in full voice and to see their flags flying. As a safety measure (prior to May Day) he orders all UN personnel out of the compounds still open—which means temporary gate clinics for several other compounds, and a few hours of scurrying around.

Before noon, more troops from the —th move in and take up positions next to FOUR, on the plateau above THREE. The already quadrupled perimeter guard is now tripled again; machine guns are set up outside the compounds (facing in) and more tanks patrol the perimeter roads.

Don't think it had anything to do with the morning visitor (it probably came from Tokyo), but someone up in the chain of command, we hear, is upset that our freshly telephoned figures of yesterday include a number of Communist prisoners listed as "absent sick," and I explain over the sputtering field phone that we've sent a handful of PWs diagnosed as having leprosy to a leper colony forty-odd miles away, and that there was little likelihood they'd leave, for they knew they'd get an unfriendly reception anywhere else. Nevertheless we are ordered to consider it urgent business that we establish head count and positive identification by personal check —which turns out to be easier—and safer—to do than to do head counting in our own backyard, where we have no idea how many are alive and how many are dead, and who is who.

Since there are lots of jeeps with nothing to do at the moment, I take Mr. Chang, my interpreter, and Lt. Gregory, one of the new doctors, while Sgt. Klinghoffer drives and brings along fingerprinting pads. We follow the bumpy substitute for a road northeast above ELEVEN, past the tanks and half-tracks, up hills and down into small villages. Then up steeper hills, until lovely panoramas appear below: terraced rice paddies on the slopes, a patchwork of flat rice paddies beyond; circular, thatch-roofed huts gathered together in village clusters; thin blue rivulets; and at the top of the most bare, rocky peaks are scattered, scrubby little trees, making small green patches on the gray crags. In little clumps here and there are pinkish-violet cherry blossoms.

The familiar thought returns: how beautiful Korea looks from a distance, elevation erasing the sordidness and the stench. The climb continues, and miles of rocky, narrow, dusty roads follow, descending finally into a fairly large village, which except for size and an air of being untouched by recent events (the color of olive drab is conspicuously missing), looks like all the others. We pass the familiar thatched huts; men, oxen, and women (in that order of local value) working in the fields, not lifting their eyes to the sound of the putt-putt of the jeep; children playing in the road or running after our vehicle; a fragrant honey cart moving slowly along the road, causing Sgt. Klinghoffer to slow down and inch warily around the traveling fumes.

In the village proper the inhabitants watch us go by,

dulled eyes widening in their peculiarly seamed and scarred faces. "This must be it," says Gregory loudly (then in a whisper to me, adding, "You know, I've never seen a leper before!").

"Kyeng Sang Nam," confirms Mr. Chang. But his identification is hardly needed, for although most people we see evidence no serious lesions, I see among the gathering knot of curious villagers one without a nose, one without fingers, and some with flesh in other places eroded by leprosy. The half-dozen PWs in residence trot forward in their GI clothes, the best-dressed inhabitants of Kyeng Sang Nam. The interrogation is over quickly, and fingerprints taken of all available fingers, when someone chatters to Mr. Chang in high-pitched, rapid Korean.

"He says there is one more PW, and he will go and get him."

Soon the villager returns, followed by a sturdy, stocky little fellow in green GI fatigues with "PW" daubed in black on the worn knees, and on the back of his jacket. Behind come more curious people, all the village apparently now swarming around to listen to us check personal data and acquire a new set of fingerprints of Kim Kee Yong. Since Lt. Gregory doesn't, I ask him where he is sick, for he appears hearty and happy; and he points to a lesion on his lower lip. Checking his records I discover that he is seven days older than I am—we were both twenty-three this month.

On our own we make a tour of the village, the curious dispersing as we go, the children returning to their games in the dust of the main road. It is a surprise to discover how self-supporting the village is, even though most of the population are lepers (the others their families). They till their own fields, make their own clothes, and furnish their own huts, supplying all their own wants but medicines, which come irregularly from outside. They fish in the Japan Sea, nearby, and cut timber in the hills overlooking the village. And sensible of their common bond, they live cooperatively and at peace with one another, no barriers of ideology interfering with the Communist prisoners' happy adjustment to life there. For them—their initial horror of their disease diluted by its commonness in the village—it is an earthly paradise, and I cannot imagine their wanting to be repatriated to a Communist utopia.

From the village it is a short walk to the sea. Less than a quarter mile away is a rocky promontory looking out over the calm water—a royal blue in the bright sunlight. The deep purple crags rise high above the sea, and in the inlet far below we see fishermen with nets and lines and in their boats a respectable day's catch—dark, wriggling masses of squid. Thoughts of prisoners and hospitals and war temporarily recede—something we fail to realize until we hear the distant honking of the jeep's horn, reminding us that we must make the trip back in full daylight.

Sgt. Klinghoffer, we discover, has been dozing in the driver's seat and has slumped forward on the horn, elbowing it and waking himself up with a start. We commend his alertness with as much sarcasm as we can, and with no enthusiasm whatever we head back.

Re-entering the enclosure, I'm informed by the sentry-post corporal, "They've been looking all over for you, sir. There's a big shipment of patients reported due any-time now." At midnight they arrive, the first cases in three weeks to arrive from Koje: 480 screened-South PWs. They enter on huge, open trailer trucks, singing South Korean songs and waving ROK flags. We hold our breath, for they're due to pass the closed Communist compounds and anything could happen. But the U.S. troops guarding the convoy force the South Koreans to quiet down, put away the flags and banners, and at least *appear* docile. There is no trouble, although by this time the awakened PWs in every ward have clustered by the fences to watch.

Patient processing goes quickly, and the PWs, once safe within South wards, break out their banners. With every-thing going routinely, I join Capt. Valentine on his nightly ride around the outer perimeter. All is quiet at 0100—and it is actually May Day already, we realize. Reaching the first of the neighboring villages, we hesi-tate entering. The blackness is unappealing, and we turn back.

Back at my hut an appalling sight greets me on the sack as I go to turn in: three weeks' worth of *The New York Times* arrived today (the most recent issue four weeks old), about two thousand pages.

Interlude—The World Outside

We knew, by the end of April, 1952, that we were engaged in two wars in Korea which we could not possibly win. We could not attack the sources of Communist military power in China without risking the alienation of all of our United Nations allies and risking as well the massive intervention of Russia. We could not even use our crushing power to win the secondary war behind our own lines—to quell the prisoner mutinies against screening and restore law and order—without both endangering the lives of anti-Communist prisoners and affecting our posture before the world as the upholder of the decencies of law and order in war. As an additional frustration, our own men, held as prisoners by the Communists, were hostages to any agreement with the Communists.

On April 28, 1952, the UN armistice negotiators headed by Admiral C. Turner Joy had submitted to the Communists what they called their final package proposal. It modified our position on certain other matters but held firm to the principle of voluntary repatriation. General Nam Il, the chief Communist negotiator, was equally adamant about the prisoner question. Although he knew better from his efficient spy apparatus in the prison camps, he professed the convenient fiction that the term voluntary *was nonsense: no North Korean or Chinese prisoner of war would have* voluntarily *rejected Communism. At the truce tent in Panmunjom he summed up, during one of his standard tirades, the Communist propaganda line which had stalled any agreement on ending the war:*

> *Everybody knows that for a long period of time you have been using Chiang Kai-shek's gangsters and Syngman Rhee's agents to take all kinds of barbarous measures to coerce our captured personnel into refusing repatriation. You have not hesitated to use methods of bloodshed and murder to gain your infamous aim. . . .*
>
> *In order to assist you to gain the aim of retaining our captured personnel, the Chiang Kai-shek ring repeatedly directed their agents to force our captured personnel to start the so-called movement of refusing repatriation by writing blood petitions, making appeals, and even by announcing collective suicide. For all these facts, our side is in possession of incontestable evidence. Your activities in employing barbarous methods in an attempt to retain our captured personnel by force have already reached such an extent as makes it impossible for you to hide or deny them.*
>
> *To strengthen your rule of bloodshed and violence over our captured personnel, your side recently moved large amounts of reinforcing forces to the locality of your prisoner-of-war camp, for further sup-*

*pression of the just resistance of our captured person-
nel. The fact now placed before the people of the
whole world is that in spite of your such barbarous
measures, you violated the will of the captured personnel of our side. Thousands of them would rather
die than yield to your forcible retention. Your side
dares not face this fact. In order to cover up this fact,
your side has invented the myth that our captured
personnel were not willing to be repatriated.*

Of course Nam Il said nothing about the ideological
intimidation of the dwindling numbers of UN troops
held captive by the Communists. Once claiming sixty-five
thousand prisoners, they had submitted to the truce negotiators names of less than twelve thousand. The explanation that the rest had been "released at the front"
masked two lies. The Communists probably had never
had that many prisoners, except for purposes of their
propaganda broadcasts; and most of the Koreans they
had captured early in the war had been impressed into
their own armies, whether or not they had actually been
soldiers in the first place.

Meanwhile, as General Nam certainly knew, Communist "indoctrination" of UN—especially U.S.—captured
personnel had been proceeding remarkably well. The
only difficulty as of April 30, 1952, lay in extorting confessions of bacteriological warfare from American fliers.
Since early winter the Chinese had been exploiting
charges—ludicrously flimsy frauds for which they had
achieved such wide currency that even the Chinese were
taken by surprise—that American planes had been in-
fecting China by germ raids of diseased bugs, rats, clams,

and flies. The bizarre propaganda hoax had obscure origins. It may have been intended at first only to conceal the embarrassing fact that typhus had arrived in the Korean peninsula from Manchuria when the Chinese had intervened. So spectacularly had the hoax succeeded that it became necessary to produce genuine American bacterial bombers; but four months of solitary confinement and ceaseless interrogation of two American Air Force officers could not achieve a May Day propaganda coup of a confession. (The first "confessions" finally came on May 5.)

This Soviet-style brainwashing was the exception made necessary by circumstance and by unusual American resistance. For the most part, particularly with American enlisted men, Communist "indoctrination" was a subtle system. It involved no application of macabre tortures, but instead utilized unmelodramatic mental and physical pressures. Humiliating a man before his peers or isolating him for long periods, withholding substantial food, or medicines and hospital care, often had more efficient results than threats of bodily harm. What if the short-waved greetings to relatives back home included a few obligatory words of Red propaganda? Wasn't it a small price to pay for letting them know one was alive? What harm did signing peace or surrender petitions do if one needed medical care or a better diet? What if one attended daily—and lengthy—indoctrination classes in Communism? After all, in the monotony of prison camp existence, a man had to do something, didn't he? Besides, didn't the political instructor have the authority to order or to mitigate punishment? Or to make it easier for one

112

Published by PEACE NEWS PRESS

No. 3   KOREA   NOVEMBER, 1952

Our Camp Hospital

I am writing this letter for all those who came here with me to this camp hospital. We had many men who were very near death, wounded and sick when captured. When we came here we were received warmly by the hospital staff. There was hot food to eat and bedding provided for us. The hospital staff started giving us medical care immediately upon our arrival.

The next day we were provided with three hot meals which were similar to our own American food. We were given strawberry jam, sugar, bread and tobacco. Also many other things we had not seen for many months. Every morning when we wake, a nurse comes around and gives us all a glass of warm milk.

Our daily menu consists of either beef, pork, or chicken. We also are given a variety of fresh vegetables.

The men who were so sick that they were expected to die were given the best of medical care available, and also a special diet of four to six meals a day.

The doctors and nurses are looking in on us every few minutes day and night and medicine is given at all hours around the clock.

We are now all on the road to recovery and some of us are getting fat. I, myself am very fat and healthy now.

I want to thank all the hospital staff and the Chinese People's Volunteers for their great lenient policy toward prisoners and for treating them as their own fellow men.

North Korea published this POW "newspaper," showing the world how serene conditions were on the other side of the battle line.

News From Your POW Buddies

My Impressions Of POW Life

Since I was captured I have learned numerous things about the Chinese People's Volunteers. To begin with, when I stepped upon the road, with hands raised above my head and surrendered. I had heard good stories about them but I had heard many more horrifying rumors which originated from higher rank and was handed down to the fighting men in the fox holes. Upon being captured I was very astonished when the Volunteers motioned me to lower my hands and then in turn began to shake my hand.

Since my capture and up to now I've witnessed many actual happenings which definitely prove that the Volunteers are truly trying to improve our living conditions as much as possible.

Our living quarters are well papered, beds have been constructed for our comfort and shelves for our personal belongings. Our chow consists of a much wider variety than ever before, such as fresh pork, fresh tomatoes, egg plant, cabbage, eggs, squash and fresh fish. Besides, we have sufficient ration of both sugar and tobacco.

Organized athletics are in full swing in the various camps giving all of us an equal opportunity to compete in such sports as basketball, softball and volleyball and we had track and field events also. The Volunteers issued prizes to winning teams and outstanding individuals in athletics to give us a goal to work for.

Men, doesn't such humane treatment prove to you all that we are truly in the care of real friends? Well I fully realize it and greatly appreciate it.

Pilot A Prisoner; Wife Is Happy

A UP dispatch from Wynnewood, Pennsylvania, says that Mrs. Emily Heller 29, wife of 2nd Lt. Edwin L. Heller, a Sabrejet pilot, was "jubilant" over the news that her husband was reported a prisoner of the Chinese Communists after his plane was shot down on Jan. 23.

UP reported from Tokyo on Jan. 27 that 2nd Lt. James Lovely, a fellow pilot of Lt. Heller's, was astonished and happy when he heard Heller was safe and a prisoner.

"What!" exclaimed Lovely, "That's wonderful! I'll be darned. That's fine."

Note: On Jan. 23, 1953, a Sabrejet of the U.S. Air Force was brought down in Northeast China. The pilot, 2nd Lt. Edwin L. Heller was captured by the Chinese People's Air Force. His wife and children live in Wynnewood, Pa.

Published in *Peace*, March 1, 1953, these articles were accompanied by photographs of smiling POWs and their North Korean captors. The captions: "Music and songs"; "Letters from home come often."

to get medical treatment, or even to recommend the nature—and severity—of one's camp maintenance duties? Thus was integrity eroded in the mass.

The prisoner death rate among the Americans, it was later discovered, was 38 per cent. This was due partly to a fatal American fastidiousness about eating unfamiliar Oriental food, and partly to rampaging dysentery among the Americans trapped by the Chinese intervention. But hospital care was no more Western than were the daily rations of rice, cabbage, half-cooked soya beans, and millet.

A typical Communist medical facility for prisoners was the hospital for Americans at the Yalu River town of Pyoktong, in North Korea. In happier days it had been a Buddhist monastery. The Chinese supervisory doctors were appointed on the basis of their political reliability, rather than their ability to treat—or even to recognize— anything beyond superficial physical symptoms. New inmates were regularly brought in to replace the dead, maintaining the patient population at about one hundred. By April, 1952, there was somewhat less lice and filth in the hospital than during the first year of the war, and medication and diet had improved. There were no longer ten deaths a day, although few days passed without some deaths.

On May 1, 1952, accustomed to the compliance of many American prisoners of war, the Communists administering one camp in North Korea provided Red banners and badly needed new uniforms, and blandly informed the Americans that the new issue and the banners were for marching in the parade. A few prisoners

115

urgently passed the word that no one was to fall out for the parade, "no matter what." Not even the most timid prisoners risked collaborating in the face of such organized mass resistance, and the puzzled Communists retaliated by placing a few suspected instigators in stockade. But there was no parade in camp that May Day.

May 1, 1952–May 22, 1952

May Day turns out to be sunny, warm, and spectacularly beautiful—the hills have lost their dingy aspect. The order of the day to security personnel is the familiar one, but reiterated for May Day: no shooting except in cases of breakout. Demonstrations to be tolerated as usual. ONE celebrates at sunrise (not giving me much sleep) with a colorful pageant, featuring huge portraits of Mao, Kim Il Sung, and Stalin, plus other Communist saints I can't identify. Possibly the bald-headed Communist is Lenin, although Oriental in the local artist's conception. The prisoners march around the compound with paper floral wreaths, flags, and banners emblazoned with propaganda. SEVEN—unimaginative—continues with its usual flag waving, singing, and marching. Neighborly TWO reciprocates with a regimental parade, a good deal of singing of the too familiar North Korean Red Army song, dozens of North Korean, Chinese, and Russian flags, and a smart bit of close-order drill. The May Day parade in THREE is similar but with more embellishments. PWs there climb on their hut roofs to display propaganda banners—even one in English, which advises: "AMERICANS! GO BACK TO YOUR HAPPY HOMES. YOUR FAMILIES DO NOT WANT YOU TO DIE INVADING OTHER LANDS." The noise continues well into the afternoon, with the passion of the demonstrations in the other compounds far inferior to that of THREE and TWO.*

At night the Communists in THREE begin to taper off. They had been going with the same gusto all day, possibly working in shifts. All the other compounds are quiet.

As Officer of the Day, I have to sit up in headquarters (or at least sleep there all night) waiting for something to happen. Nothing vital does, but this affords lots of time for paging through the *Times*. Three weeks' worth is a full night's work. It's amazing how important the unimportant things in a paper become when one reads them at a distance halfway around the world and after a lapse of a month or so. I now read items I never would have looked at had I been reading the paper on the date of issue. I read all the ads, the local news of a state I've never lived in, stale news about a city I've merely visited (for that matter, I even read Lt. Knox's home-hamlet weekly), trivial news about people of whom I've never heard getting married or buried, and (most exciting of all) ads and reviews of plays and movies that may have already closed by the time I get the paper. Some-

---

* In a futuristic fantasy about the absurd horrors of Communism, Polish satirist Slawomir Mrozek has a Communist radio announcer describe the tag end of a May Day parade: "We can already hear the noise of stamping and shuffling," he reports enthusiastically. "Yes, here they come. Our glorious incomparable rehabilitated invalids. A spirited detachment of legless men who are swinging their crutches with gusto. Wooden legs reflect the sun. Two men who have lost an arm each get together so they can clap." (*The Elephant*, New York: Grove Press, 1963) Looking at these lines from the perspective of my Korean notes of April and May, 1952, I find the future not entirely *ahead* of us. (See also p. 155.)

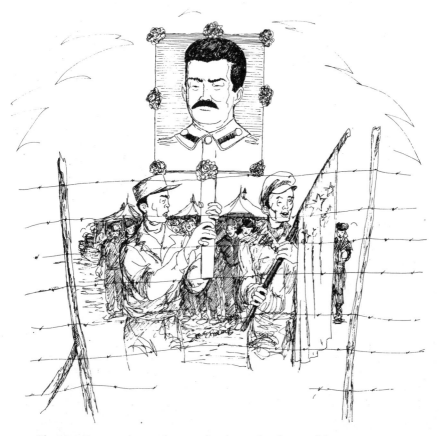

The May Day parade...with paper floral wreaths, flags, and banners emblazoned with propaganda.

one drifts in on routine business and gazes thoughtfully at my excuse for activity.

"This will never replace living," he says.

The medical business is almost nonexistent, and I ask the yawning Medical Officer of the Day, who is snuggling under his blanket, "Huey, shall I wake you for breakfast?"

"Yeah, Stan, except if I'm asleep."

It's quiet at dawn. At 0800 I turn over the O.D. honor to the new day's stand-in and have breakfast. Everyone thinks I'm crazy because I still like scrambled powdered eggs and fried Spam for breakfast. They've been threatening to have one of our neurologists look me over, but I remind them that medics attached to this hospital may practice only PW medicine.

A big sick call surprisingly materializes at the TWO gate clinic, even though it's raining lightly. But the patients in THREE still remain stubborn. At 1400 the *honcho* in TWO discovers that one of his people, on getting through the gate for treatment, has pleaded for asylum. When the PW doesn't return on his demand, the *honcho* stops releasing patients, and the dispensary's business dries up. But that's one hostage less.

Confusion or no, our monthly reports have to go out —even though no one has been close enough to many of the patients for weeks to be able to count them, let alone check on their condition. But we project figures, and the finished reports insanely suggest business as usual, for there's no place in them for anything but numbers.

I'm beginning to wonder whether May Day wasn't a dud for the Communists. Even we are taking each new demonstration as anticlimax after the frenzied activity of the earlier ones. It must be more difficult now for the monitors to whip up a frenzy, especially since those actually sick aren't getting any better. Maybe this is why the gate-clinic business is picking up, in spite of exhortations from the PW leadership not to patronize this hospital substitute.

The rain lifts a little and some clear sky shows through, giving Capt. Jerry Leiper the idea that the best cure for severe claustrophobia is not alcohol (he's tried that—as has everyone—with only spotty results) but mountain climbing. He's from Colorado and has nothing but scorn for those of us who call the local hills "mountains." It's still early enough in the day to get started, he suggests to all the bored surgeons, but all of them point out that the hills are supposed to be full of guerrillas, and that we've been officially discouraged from leaving the dubious safety of our barbed wire during the emergency situation. But the clear interval is tantalizing, and my taste of the outside still recent. I volunteer to go along, since I don't have to be on duty the afternoon following my O.D. stint.

A newly arrived warrant officer, Ed Garraty, not yet assigned to duty, decides to join us; and Lt. Bill Boyle, a compound C.O. currently without a compound to administer, also agrees to go. Between us, we take a .45 pistol and two carbines for moral support (I'm the exception without a weapon). The hill we pick is the closest to us, the major prominence overlooking the camp, and affectionately known, because of its shape, as "Mooseteat." I don't even know any other name for it, but assume it has one.

Halfway up the hill Ed and I are about to give up and return, but think the better of it for lack of courage.

Panting heavily and aching of foot, we straggle slightly behind, while Bill and Jerry clamber ahead, calling to us now and then, "C'mon, you mountain goats!"

There is a small temple on the side of the hill, with mounds near it where some once wealthy Koreans lay buried (the higher on a hill, I'm told, the higher one's former position in society). The wooden columns of the little Buddhist sanctuary are faded and weather-worn and decorated with portraits in bas-relief of gargoylish-looking Buddhas. From the temple the camp looks insignificantly small. None of our armored vehicles circling it or perched on prominences overlooking it is visible.

At the summit we find a large grave mound, unmarked but probably the last resting place of a very prosperous and important citizen. Sitting on the mound, we can see as far as the Sea of Japan on one side, and far in the distance on another is the gray, dingy, sprawling city of Pusan, on the edge of a many-fingered bay. To the north are tiny clusters of villages and the long valley to Taegu, flanked by forest-covered hills of deep green. Barely visible to the west, where rain clouds are beginning to gather again, are the threadlike runways of an airbase, with jet trails in the sky above it getting fuzzy and fading into the returning mist.

Worried about getting caught in rain or dusk, we begin to work our way down again, muscles in our calves aching with each step, the rain-loosened soil and rock crumbling underfoot here and there. "Nob Hill" nearby comes into view around one turn, and Bill points to a reminder of civilization on its summit: "Isn't that the radar station that's been shot up by guerrillas a few times

126

since the last snow?" The thought spurs Ed to more rapid downward progress, and we soon find ourselves within sight of the perimeter road, hoping for a passing jeep or half-track. None appears, and in the fading light we trudge up the hill leading past the Women's Compound, and down again into the camp, feeling tired and foolish.

En route to my hut I check in to see if there's anything for me to sign, or calls to return. "Yessir," reports Sgt. Klinghoffer, "only to call your hut." Rather than crank the phone I continue down the hill and find a lone occupant, Lt. Glenn Thomas, sitting on a sack, head in his hands, several empty beer cans on the floor.

"I got orders transferring me out of here," he says, still looking at the ground.

"Going back on the line to an infantry unit, Glenn?"

"No such luck. I'm to leave for Koje-do tomorrow morning." And he begins comparing the voyage of the daily courier boat to Koje with the daily trip of Charon, the ferryman of Greek myth who transported the dead across the River Styx to Hades.

I look at a copy of his orders and exclaim that it's only an assignment to temporary duty.

"Yeah, so was this duty temporary."

At 0900, in the rain and fog, the commanding general arrives on a secret, unannounced visit. He turns up in combat fatigues, without insignia, and leaves again an hour later for a flight to Tokyo.

Some problems appear regarding the latest shipment of PWs from Koje. In checking the Koje roster, the ship manifest, and our latest admission roster, we find that no two agree, except that more PWs arrived than were supposed to. Not only were there stowaways but some patients weren't admitted because they apparently claimed to be laborers. There are at least one psycho case and one tuberculous pleurisy case wandering around loose somewhere.

Three more escapes from TWO. The *honcho* thought that this time he had screened all the gate-clinic patients for loyalty. Sgt. Cartier's escape system is working well in the TWO dispensary so far—holding back any who are reluctant to return until the entire sick call has come through the gate. But the Communists are highly peeved, and after dark break into the main admissions and dispositions area, mutilating records, equipment, and wiring, and stealing whatever movable objects remain in the dispensary hut. An object of the visit, possibly, is to look for records of the three new escapees; but no records are there any longer.

More rain, fog, and mud—a dismal morning. Despite the weather, ONE, TWO, and THREE (with SEVEN belatedly joining them) put on elaborate demonstrations of the usual variety. Even so, all but TWO allow sick call to proceed at the gate clinics, and the demonstrations decrease in intensity as the rain increases. Although some patients from ONE have been appearing for treatment, they're apparently those cleared by the *honchos* as politically safe. And the PWs there—led by the Chinese —are still protesting every aspect of their care, although they've created the situation they're in. There's a new letter from them, delivered to the sally-port guard:

> *We who desire repatriation also desire more practice of medicine in the compound.*
> *You give enough food to the SK PW and others but give us only half as much rice, and only watery soup.*
> *You have tortured those of us who were in surgery, dispatching your ugly devils who are almost murdering us.*
> *Is this the only way that you Western-style countries and Americans can treat us? We hope you stop this kind of treatment. If not, we can't tell what will happen in the future.*
> *Chinese People's Volunteers in Compound One*

One of the oddities about the rice all the PWs get— and they all get the same rations in quantity and quality —is that the huge sacks of the stuff from which we dispense their rations are labeled "Texas Rice" or "Louisiana Rice" or "Carolina Rice." At least there should be less of a rice shortage in the Far East this year, since we're feeding 180,000 PWs—and countless South Koreans—the American product.

In spite of the foul weather, we've received thirty-three new live patients and one dead on arrival. Even though Koje hasn't been sending us as many prisoners as we've expected, our sick and wounded population is still over eight thousand—8271, more or less.

The big news of the day is that Lt. Knox has received orders transferring him to Japan. His first thought is of his mint plot, and he magnanimously turns it over to the custody of the other doctors in his hut. Someone asks him whether he wouldn't like to stay on here a few more weeks to see what happens here. His answer: "No. Write me."

Work on the annex is proceeding very slowly because of the bad weather, and both men and vehicles returning from there each evening are encrusted with mud. Even here the mud is so bad now that a stroll to the latrine or to the shower shack requires boots. And the rain continues.

Chilly and wet, and the hut potbelly stove glowing, when a dismantling crew arrives to take the stove away. Although it's more like February or March at the moment, the Army works strictly by regulations, and today all units under this command must give up their winter heating devices and return them to the nearest Quartermaster supply depot. Capt. Hank Lesser, sitting on the edge of his sack, waiting for the coffee water (in the bucket on the top of the stove) to boil, is outraged by the deferential plea of the enlisted men that he give up his only creature comfort. Although they can't fathom him, his tirade really reflects frustration at being unable to practice medicine, something certainly not obvious in his "To hell with your 'please sir's!' And regulations be damned—we're keeping our stove!"

The GI crew's reaction is the feeble protest of those who know they've lost: "I'm sorry but we'll have to report this, sir." The hut keeps its stove, and a minor hold upon sanity.

We are ordered to conduct the business of the hospital as normally as possible; and told that this includes the reopening of the main Admissions and Dispositions facilities. With great reluctance I ask some of my men to move back into that uncomfortable enclave between the unscreened holdouts in TWO and the Communists squeezed into SEVEN. The enclosure is littered with filth and rubble from repeated PW invasions and vandalism, and equipment abandoned inside the huts is wrecked. Patiently the GIs clean up the old home grounds and huts while PWs cluster near the barbed wire to see what potential loot and raw materials for weapons we bring in.

In just a few hours the location proves to be no less awkward than before, for the Red PWs surrounding it on three sides soon begin a barrage of rocks and stones and debris—ostensibly at anti-Communist patients entering the enclosure for admission processing from the new screened-South mainland camps which are helping to empty Koje of all but North PWs. Nothing (under existing orders) can be done to control the PWs when the barrage gets heavy (and I get beaned too) except ask for permission to retreat shamefacedly from the area again, taking with us everything movable. Angrily, Capt. Noonan orders SEVEN closed to medical personnel because of the incident, but his punitive measure is quickly countermanded.

The nights, at least, have been quieter than we had any reason to expect.

Sunny and warm. Another battalion of the —th Regiment arrives from the line to prepare for phase two (once
all anti-Communists are evacuated)—the forced screening of ONE, TWO, and THREE, and the pacification
of SIX and SEVEN.

Early in the morning there is a meeting to iron out
final details for opening the hospital annex. I call it
(and the looks I get make it clear that others don't think
I'm taking the whole business sufficiently seriously) "Operation Day-camp"—a new 3000-bed hospital for screened-
South patients only, about seven miles away. The main
hospital area will hospitalize only PWs who wish to be
repatriated, but would take care of all major surgery,
record keeping, processing of new admissions. This will
limit friction between patients of opposing political sympathies to the pre-operative and post-operative wards,
hardly places where politics is likely to matter much to
the inmate. U.S. personnel at the annex will commute
daily from here. Thus "Day-camp."

The anti-Communists in TEN, surprisingly, are completely unaware of our plans for tomorrow—the activation
of a separate hospital area for them—and demonstrate
their uneasiness over the apparent prospect of indefinite-
term existence alongside hostile compounds. They hold
a mass meeting of all the screened-South aid-men and
patients recently transferred from Koje who remain in

the compound, and the many educated and English-speaking members of the group draft an eloquent and dramatic letter to the hospital C.O.:

6 May 1952

To Hospital Commander.
Sir,
   We . . . have done a lot of cooperating with security and medical officials, watching every kind of hateful Communist movement, cutting the secret communications sent from one Communist compound to another via the [Koje] hospital and removing the worst kind of Communists at the risk of our lives. Last February we joined the "Anti-Communist Young-Man Party of Republic of Korea" that . . . had more than forty thousand members. We solemnly created the Branch Committee of that party in the . . . hospital in the midst of the huge tide of bloody struggle between Communists and anti-Communists in Koje Island.
   We cooperated with authorities systematically through our party setup. We cannot forget the fact that many unnamed patients who honorably died fighting tough and cruel Communists as the bulwark of the free nations and Democracy were buried by our hands. We do not know how to express our cordial thanks to the . . . GIs who fully understood what we were and helped us as best they could. . . . We faithfully took care of patients and at the same time we methodically fought Communism. . . .
   We were entirely frightened and disappointed on arrival to find many Communist compounds in this

134

hospital. It is quite natural that if both Communists and anti-Communists live too closely they are liable to get each other excited. This is one of the main reasons why there had been grim, bloody riots in the POW Camp . . . of Koje Island.

We would like to work altogether in one compound of this hospital. All are absolutely faithful and loyal. . . . It is always desirable in any society that everybody has his happy job according to his knowledge and ability.

Here we firmly swear that we will do our best if this earnest hope could be materialized.

We wish you good health and further success,

Yours truly . . .

Under gray clouds "Operation Day-camp" begins. Via ambulances and trucks, screened-South PWs leave the hospital amid cheering, waving of ROK flags. The vehicles pass by hostile Communist compounds and are met by jeers and flurries of rocks.

There is tremendous confusion as patients and laborers arrive in the partially erected camp. A hot sun breaks through the clouds and begins to dry up the mud, at the same time drying and caking it on everyone and everything. The "hospital" is so new that much of it, including huts, tents, roads, sanitation facilities, and barbed-wire fencing, is still on paper. The ambulance drivers show up with their patients from the main hospital only to find that they have to halt to help build their own road to drive the ambulances up. Nevertheless, amid the chaos, a tent city begins to arise out of the rice paddies. By the end of the day all the former occupants of FOUR have been transferred to the annex. It's a good thing that it gets darker later now.

A movie is being shown in the mess hall when we return—the Technicolor Bible story, *Samson and Delilah*. The sound track is almost—but not really—as bad as the last movie, *The Philadelphia Story*. It's so frayed that it's practically a silent film. Since I know how it all comes out anyway, I go back to my hut to keep going on *The Caine Mutiny*. I have to hide the book until I finish it, for everybody wants to read it, and I've already had it nearly a week.

Screened-South PWs leave the hospital amid cheering, waving of ROK flags.

In the hut is Capt. Lewis, busy writing his wife the daily letter. He doesn't want her to worry, so he hasn't yet mentioned our local problems. He writes page after page about all the interesting cases he's seen and operations he's performed. Yet he hasn't done any surgery (except emergency stuff) in almost a month, and can't see any new surgery cases in his compound except at a great distance—it's one of the veteran holdout ones.

Some of the doctors with nothing to do most of the time now brood to each other over their most agonizing cases, now impossible to care for in the hostile compounds, and impossible even to check on. Lewis and Bullock have even taken to walking round the barbed wire surrounding ONE, hoping to spot some of the plastic-surgery cases. Their prize patient, O Soo Sik, a victim of napalm burns, has gone through many stages of skin grafting but was far from the end of them when it became impossible to do further surgery—or even to see him or change his dressings. Since then he hasn't appeared— or been permitted by the *honchos* to appear—at the gate clinic. For Lewis the suspense is unbearable. Will O Soo Sik's skin grafts slough out? Will the area beneath the long-unchanged dressings become infected? And there are other patients who have survived unbelievable disfigurement and who need continuing, gradual structural repairs now impossible. Delays may break down all of their progress to date—if they survive at all. Will O Soo Sik be shot up by us—or murdered inside by his comrades—after all the labors of Lewis and others to provide him with ears and rebuild his jaw? Why hasn't he come

139

to the gate clinic? Is he already dead, or very ill? So go the spoken and unspoken questions.

As some of us are peeling down to go to bed, the hut door flies open and a newly arrived officer pokes his head inside and shouts, "Do y'all know that this here place is on the same parallel of latitude as North Carolina?"

Lewis reaches for his boot. Heaved, it thuds against the hastily closed door. He gets up and retrieves it, then climbs in the sack.

Violent hot winds are blowing clouds of dust over the area. Under a pall of dust we manage to transfer half the occupants of TEN over the rutted "roads" to the annex. The tents being erected are blown into balloon shapes by the wind, but none blows apart, and patients are installed in them as fast as, the canvas is raised. There are all kinds of shortages and growing pains at the annex—not enough aid-men or PW doctors, not enough medical supplies on hand because of storage problems, not enough security personnel, not enough barbed wire. Even water is short.

All of us involved in the annex operation are in conference in hospital headquarters about new problems raised by the annex when a telephoned message from the area general interrupts. We're ordered to close all North compounds immediately—no reason given.

Soon the order arrives, in writing, that the commanding general "has personally directed this command that U.S. and civilian personnel are forbidden to enter the Communist compounds, effective at once. Medical care may continue to be given to prisoners who come to the compound gates for treatment. Treatment will not be given inside the compounds. In compounds where there is a sally-port, this may be used for treatment. Food will continue to be drawn in accordance with the present arrangement. . . ."

All compounds in the main hospital enclosure, except

for the anti-Communist TEN, now in process of moving, are barred to U.S. and ROK personnel, and gate clinics set up at the only two compounds the new order actually affects (the others have been all but closed anyway), SIX and FIVE. The PWs can't understand why they're being treated this way—especially FIVE, which though Communist, has been relatively cooperative. But we're still ignorant of the reason too, and tension in the enclosure increases, communicating rapidly to the PWs, who are unusually silent.

Rising wind. Dust clouds whistle through the barbed wire all afternoon.

A new confab in the evening continues the one interrupted earlier. Now we have more news: the general in command at Koje has been taken hostage by Communist prisoners. He was conferring with PWs at an open compound gate when (by prearranged plan) he was dragged inside. It was incredible that he should have placed himself in such a position, since as recently as April 29 (we now learn) the general's assistant, a lieutenant colonel, was seized while in the same compound and held for three hours before being released. This time the PWs had prepared signs painted on blankets in case their coup succeeded: "WE CAPTURE GENERAL DODD. IF OUR PROBLEMS ARE RESOLVED HIS SECURITY IS GUARANTEED. IF THERE IS BRUTAL ACT OR SHOOTING HIS LIFE IS IN DANGER."*

* The actual demands of the general's captors were so worded that any agreement to them was, in effect, an admission of the crimes alleged. Translated hastily from Korean, the incredible document read as follows:

1. Immediate ceasing the barbarous behavior, insults, torture,

142

Since the PW grapevine provides very rapid communication, our "Operation Cleanout" may have to be delayed to safeguard the general's life. And we have to consider, too, whether this bit of PW daring is part of any larger plot that concerns our situation here. Although it quite clearly has happened, everyone is walking around unbelieving—it seems too bizarre and fantastic even for this place.

The first command reaction is an order calculated to prevent any encore here. It "reminds" personnel not to enter the Communist compounds under any circumstances, and to take "personal safety measures" to insure not being taken as a hostage. Also, it warns against any communication with Communist PWs "except when absolutely necessary" and "in the line of duty only."

We hear that a tank battalion and another infantry

---

forcible protest with blood writing, threatening, confine, mass murdering, gun and machine-gun shooting, using poison gas, germ weapons, experiment object of A-bomb, by your command. You should guarantee PW human rights and individual life with the base on the International Law.

2. Immediate stopping the so-called illegal and unreasonable voluntary repatriation of North Korean Peoples Army and Chinese Peoples Volunteer Army PW.

3. Immediate ceasing the forcible investigation (screening) which thousands of PW of North Korean Peoples Army and Chinese Peoples Volunteer be rearmed and falled in slavery, permanently and illegally.

4. Immediate recognition of the PW Representative Group (Commission) consisted of North Korean Peoples Army and Chinese Peoples Volunteer Army PW and close cooperation to it by your command.

This Representative Group will turn in Brig Gen Dodd, USA, on your hand after we receive the satisfactory written declaration to resolve the above items by your command. We will wait for your warm and sincere answer.

regiment are on their way to Koje. Certainly this will deplete front-line reserves even more.

Morale is pretty low this evening. Lt. Herman spends his time erecting fiber-glass mosquito netting about his sack, although we haven't seen a mosquito yet this year. He calls it his "glass cocoon." Equally jolly is Lt. Jenks, whose comment on the atmosphere is, "We ought to call this place the House of Usher." Suddenly demon-inspired, Jenks leaps to the hut telephone and cranks it violently, shouting that he's going to cheer up the harassed medical staff on Koje with his suggestions for more effective diagnosis and treatment of incipient kidnapping, to prevent it from becoming chronic. Much confusion on the line as he gets through the Army's various code exchanges (beginning with our appropriately named hospital exchange: "Ragbag"). Finally he makes it, by which time all of the hut's occupants are gathered round, except Herman—flat on his back and silent in his cocoon—and "Spider" Biddle, who watches from a corner and polishes his metal-rimmed glasses on his sleeve.

The first collective laughter has barely gone up when the phone goes dead. Almost in unison we turn left in Spider's direction and watch him quietly put away his bandage scissors and crawl into the sack, pulling his blankets up over his head. The party breaks up, without lynching even being discussed.

TEN completes its move to the annex in cool, sunny weather: the atmosphere is pleasant—almost pastoral in its placidity. As each tent goes up, an ambulance unloads patients to fill it. Security is informal—a vast contrast to the situation just seven miles south. Barbed wire is still being strung around the annex. In the distance its first occupants (the ambulatory ones) roam about the hillsides picking wild flowers. One PW, I hear, came back from a stroll and presented a beautiful bouquet to Lt. Baer, his ward doctor. Awed and surprised, Baer asked where such pretty flowers were to be found, having been too busy to notice anything but the surrounding rice paddies—and those via their unflowerlike fragrance. "Up on that hill," said the PW, pointing to a formidable-looking peak in the distance, far beyond the half-strung fence. He's one of well over two thousand patients we moved here in the last three days, plus some additional hundreds of PW hospital attendants. Not many more of either category are expected from the three holdout compounds: we assume that they're at least 95 per cent Communist.

Today again, out of regard for the captive general's health, plans for forced screening have been delayed. Now we hear that they've been delayed indefinitely. The great unspoken elation in the closed compounds seems a clear sign to us that the news of the Koje kidnapping has leaked in. The PWs in the amputee ward in THREE seem no longer able to contain their glee, and—for the first time since screening toubles began—organize a volleyball game. They play with amazing dexterity, in spite of their loss of limbs, and the more disabled patients gather on the sidelines to cheer. But the cheering brings us, and they stop the game and refuse to perform while we watch. We stay, and after some minutes of silence they decide not to outwait us, and grimly return to their huts. Silently, we leave too.

Late in the day my telephone rings, and Cpl. Alfieri hands it to me with a note of urgency in his voice: "It's for you, sir. A Major Dobson. He's got to talk to you personally." I pick up the phone and discover that the excited major is from the 4th Finance Disbursing Office (which sends me my salary on the last day of each month). If I don't sign my name on the payroll sheet more legibly next time, he threatens, I won't get paid.

I resist (since he's a major) telling him that there's nothing here to spend it on anyway, but can't resist asking whether it would be all right to print my name. No, he says, for that's not a signature and could easily be forged.

"Yessir," I reply.

The urgent call is concluded, and I explain to my bewildered GIs what the strange conversation was all about: they've delayed leaving for the chow line to find out.

My usually illegible signature *has* disintegrated completely and gets worse (if that's possible) after each batch of PW Geneva Convention "Proof of Death" certificates are processed, for I have to sign each copy in several places, and eight copies for each PW, besides each accompanying form. For a while, when I first got here, I had a second-lieutenant assistant employed almost full-time preparing, signing, and disposing of the "Proof of Death" forms, there were so many to handle, including the dead on arrival, many of them just identified as "unknown Chinese" (or Korean). Now that Lt. Marsh has gone on to more interesting work somewhere forward, I have to sign my name a lot more—perhaps 150 to 200 times every day. Can't imagine anything more depressing to put one's name to.

SIX is a nuisance again, its leadership refusing to permit PWs there to accept treatment offered at the gate clinic set up when the compound was declared out of bounds. They haven't done anything themselves to warrant the suspension of hospital care, yet we have to treat them in the same way as those PWs who have been holding out against screening. The compound *honcho* blusters at the sally-port with a fist-shaking entourage, and threatens to create incidents "beyond the vision of U.N. forces" rather than "die slow death of illness." Ironically, all the patients in SIX are dying slow deaths of illness, no matter what we do, for all the patients there are in advanced stages of tuberculosis, the Korean national disease. And all we can do for the most part is slow down the progress of the disease.

A squadron of light planes—L-19s—flies overhead, carrying Far East high-command personnel to a conference on Koje-do.

Late at night—nearly midnight—a conspiracy is hatched by the officers of a hut across from us (and

147

abetted by us) to kidnap Lt. Anderson's statue. Three surgeons from the Navy surgical team, the company C.O. of the enlisted detachment of medics, and Capt. Jerry Leiper, pool tools and pry off one side of the locked wooden chest, and substitute for "Narcissus" two helmets wrapped in a blanket and taped together. Then Leiper, who has access to all the plaster because of his job (orthopedic surgeon), is boosted up to the roof of the latrine, where he plasters the bust firmly to the most obvious corner. Sometime during the night Anderson is expected to pass by, because he's O.D. A sentry passes and salutes us all. We return it with exaggerated smartness.

A sudden torrential rain breaks up the plastering party and lasts the night, providing cover for two patients—from TWO and FIVE—to escape. They had been held hostage, they say. But since FIVE *had* been screened, the PW from there is a puzzle—until we discover that he had changed his mind about going back and decided to screen South the hard way.

Rain, mud, and fog. The statue is discovered, perched forlornly on the latrine roof in the pouring rain, looking as if it is weeping rainy tears, water cascading down its face. Andy is furious.

We're directed to draw up new plans for forced screening and the discharge of patients and nonpatient PWs from the holdout compounds. The same operation will be utilized to effect both political and medical screening. Happily, we learn that coercion by withholding rations has been approved as a preliminary step, in the hope that it will inhibit resistance.

Each compound (ONE, TWO, and THREE) is to be treated as a separate military operation. Sessions of officers planning how "Cleanout" is to be run drag on into the rainy evening, with almost everyone hoping none of the elaborate plans will be needed.

News of the general's release at Koje comes over the Voice of America before it becomes officially known here. The terms of the ransom are not yet known, but extravagant rumors fly, and we wonder whether our plans will undergo alteration even before we have any opportunity to put them into effect. The Communist radio is already trumpeting about the "admissions" we've made (a price of the release) that we haven't given PWs humane treatment, that we've wantonly murdered PWs, and that we'd already forcibly screened prisoners. Worst of all, now that we've apparently been given the green light this

149

morning to prepare for forcible screening, the Red broadcasts proclaim that victorious PWs on Koje have gained our promise that no screening of any kind—nominal or forcible—will be attempted.*

I'm O.D. tomorrow.

* Dodd's replacement as commandant at Koje, another army general, ransomed Dodd by signing a statement which said in effect that we had terrorized and forcibly screened prisoners. The document was as worthless as it was false, but provided the Communists with another propaganda holiday. It read, in part, as follows:

1. . . . I do admit that there have been instances of bloodshed where many prisoners of war have been killed and wounded by UN Forces. I can assure you that in the future the prisoners of war can expect humane treatment in this camp according to the principles of International Law. . . .

2. Reference your Item 2 regarding voluntary repatriation of NKPA and CPVA prisoners of war, that is a matter which is being discussed at Panmunjom. I have no control or influence over the decisions at the Peace Conference.

3. Regarding your Item 3 pertaining to forcible investigation (screening), I can inform you that after Gen. Dodd's release, unharmed, there will be no more forcible screening or any rearming of prisoners of war in this camp, nor will any attempt be made at nominal screening. . . .

A warm, sticky morning, and the mud all about stays gluey until our boots seem twice their weight. At 0800 —breakfast rations to the compounds having been delayed temporarily—THREE is given a sound-truck-delivered ultimatum: all PWs are to assemble in a designated sector of the compound (to be screened) within one hour or their food and water will be cut off. The few PWs who have left their quarters to listen go back inside, and by 0900 no such movement has been made. Rations remain undelivered.

TWO is given the same ultimatum at 0900, and again at the end of an hour there is no attempt to comply. The sound truck moves off to ONE to deliver the same order to assemble, and again there is no response but silence and inactivity.

By this time it is nearly noon, and the compounds begin to show signs of resistance of a more overt sort, for bands of PWs, appearing sullen and defiant, begin to cruise back and forth along the fences of ONE and TWO, watching rations get delivered to SEVEN. THREE does the unexpected: there PWs begin to gather as they had been directed nearly four hours before, and there seems to be only a scattered rumbling of discontent. No flags remain on display in THREE, little singing or shouting; and although their mood is puzzling, it is gratifying. Meanwhile the —th Regiment's 1st Battalion has encircled THREE and stands ready to move in, and hospital personnel stand by in readiness to move in and medically screen each PW after he makes his decision regarding repatriation. The Registrar team will discharge all known agitators except the extremely ill, sending all discharges to Koje.

Through the noon hour the assembling proceeds slowly. By 1300 we smell a rat: the PWs are refusing to take their belongings, medical records, and identity tags with them. Not only would this make both medical and political screening impossible; it would be the same kind of coercion attempted earlier in neighboring compound SIX— to keep tabs on those who want to leave the compound in order to stay South. The Communist monitors refuse screening on any but their terms, which—as they argue —become hardened more and more into agreeing to move *en masse* but without political segregation. As the apparent agreement disintegrates into defiant stances on both sides, the mass of PWs who had assembled melts away, the prisoners dispersing into their huts, hobbling and chattering.

The infantrymen are waved off the compound perimeter and, containing their puzzlement, trot off in quiet order while the PWs in TWO silently look on. Only in ONE is there any reaction—there the PWs begin posting signs they must have been busy making all through the forenoon. In English, Chinese, and Korean, and set up near the compound sally-port, they read defiantly: "WE REFUSE TO BE INTERROGATED. WE DESIRE TO SEND A SPOKESMAN TO THE TRUCE TALKS AT PANMUNJOM." The same line is being given by the rebellious PW compounds on Koje, which shows how effective the Communist communications system must be.

Twilight is accompanied by much singing and shouting from the holdout compounds, now that the day has passed without any delivery of rations to them. The starve-out program is not airtight: adjacent compounds to THREE and TWO—SIX and SEVEN—can supply the holdouts from their own rations, at least under cover of darkness. ONE has no such source, but it has running water we can't shut off from outside. Soon it will be seen whether the Communists in the compounds receiving rations will practice their own doctrine of sharing by helping to feed their brother PWs while living on reduced rations.

Cynically, an M.P. lieutenant tells me his doubts about the operation: "All we're doing is giving Moscow another propaganda weapon. They don't care if these people starve to death: they might even order them to. Besides, the PWs must have been hoarding food secretly ever since the trouble started, and can probably go on for more weeks than the propaganda licking we'll take can stand."

I'm grateful for any positive action, and tell him so, but he refuses to consider this. "Just wait until Moscow radio picks this up," he insists.

My O.D. tour of the area reveals that the PWs in TWO are painting their hut roofs with messages and slogans. It's too dark to read them.

The clouds are slowly gliding past the moon as I retire to headquarters building; but when I lower myself into a cot, blessing the stillness, the crack of a series of shots in disorderly succession send me flying out into the direction of the noise. At the officers' huts I discover the cause: a dozen or so frustrated officers have been firing at the moon. The moon unscathed, I go back to my cot.

Lt. (U.S.N.R.) George Broome wakes me up as he reports in to be the new Medical Officer of the Day. Stunned, I realize that he is wearing a combination uniform—outlandish even for Korea—of Japanese sandals, tennis socks, green "field" pants, no hat, and a khaki shirt partly unbuttoned, exposing a huge, cavernous navel—and also the fact that he is wearing no underwear.

"You can't go in to the Colonel that way," I tell him.

"This is no hospital ship," is his answer, and in he goes.

(The Colonel is somewhat perturbed by the informality of some of the Naval officers with us on detached service, but has no complaint whatever about their high professional abilities.)

Departing headquarters for breakfast, I see that the rising sun has uncovered a tremendous painting job by the PWs in TWO: each hut roof is painted in white letters (apparently with a mixture of barley, cast plaster, and water—perhaps a clue to the extent of food stocks inside). The contrast of the letters to the ebony, tarred roofs is sharp and impressive. The slogans are in English and Korean:

"STOP THE UNLAWFUL SCREENING. . . . WE WANT RICE. . . . [next to a turned-off water outlet inside the compound] WE WANT RICE AND WATER. . . . TAKE BLAME FOR DEATH OF PATIENTS. . . ."

SEVEN has a sign displayed loyally: "GIVE FOOD TO 1, 2, 3."

154

ONE raises still-damp, blood-red flags—authentically blood-red, as whole blood seems to have been used. Not their own (or that of hostages), as we first fear. Capt. Lewis recalls that pints of it were abandoned in the supply hut there in the last hasty evacuation. As the flags dry in the sunlight, their bright red color darkens, making them not nearly as interesting in the long run as the merthiolate-dyed banners.

The marching, singing, screaming, and flag waving continues through the afternoon, with a vigor hardly indicative of any drastic alteration in the PWs diet. THREE performs intricate drill formations, despite the fact that some of those in the line of march walk with crutches, artificial limbs, and leg casts. The PWs in TWO and THREE then begin chanting alternate lines of some Communist threat as they mass at the fences adjacent to the broad dirt road which separates them. Two of the PWs in TWO hold a big banner which reads: "TAKE AWAY LAWLESS INDIVIDUAL INVESTIGATION ABOUT US." On the roof of the food preparation hut in THREE—an ironic place for it—a less literate Communist PW has lettered: "TAKE THE RESPONSIBIL-ITY OF DEATH OF PATIENTS FROM HUNGLY." TWO also has big placards on which is printed in English an open letter to us:

DEAR ALL UN SOLDIERS:
    IT IS THE RESPONSIBILITY OF YOUR AD-
MINISTRATORS TO CARE FOR POW. THEIR
CRUEL SAVAGE TREATMENT IS A VIOLATION
OF THE GENEVA CONVENTION AND MORE
INHUMAN THAN HITLER.

Wondering whether Peking or Moscow has already received—and put to use—news of the withholding of rations, we tune in the hut short-wave radio. Only the usual stuff—they're too busy concentratng on the Koje incident.

An inconspicuous visitor was here today—the commanding general of our forces in Korea. It was a brief stop to see how the new tactics are working—so brief that few knew about it.

The compounds quiet down early tonight, exhausted from demonstrating and perhaps from curtailed rations. The gate clinics are still technically open, but just about no one has used them.

The sun is shining brilliantly through a pall of haze and dust as we trudge up the hill past SEVEN, TWO, and ONE to have our breakfast and then to check on new developments. ONE and THREE are alive with new signs, mainly stressing our inhumane treatment. THREE's most interesting new banner features a slogan that we, itching to get this mess over with, endorse:

"IT WOULD BE BETTER THAT YOU SHOOT TO DEATH US THAN STARVE TO DEATH. WE WILL FIGHT YOU TO THE LAST DROP OF OUR BLOOD."

The catch to their pose is that guards at dusk yesterday (not empowered to do anything about it) have seen bucketfuls of cooked rice passed through the fence from SIX to THREE, so we know they're not going without food. TWO has a similar source. ONE doesn't, but we can't shut their water off from the outside as we did for TWO and THREE. Lesson number 1001 for the planning of the next PW camp for the next war.

The tension has now infected the pre-op and post-op wards, which we thought were insulated from agitation. One PW staggers out of the post-op hut to tell a doctor that he's feeling better and wants to leave for the annex. He looks terrible—shouldn't even be up, as he's just had emergency intestinal surgery. The real reason for his anxiety, he finally admits, is that there are too many Reds in post-op and he's scared—for they plot aloud, even when flat on their backs at distant ends of the Quonset hut.

On returning the PW to his hut we find another patient is surprisingly up and around. Hobbling about, trying to foment trouble, is a Communist PW. He carries his intravenous bottles and tubing in both hands, absorbing nourishment and disgorging hate at the same time. His fanaticism sustains him.

We got a rare communication today, transmitted through ROK sources—a letter to a prisoner from his father in Seoul. I asked Mr. Chang to translate it for me before it was delivered to make sure it was genuine, or at least appeared so. In Chang's version it came out like this:

> *Dear Son:*
>
> *We have worried about you since you had been dragged away by the cruel puppet [i.e., North Korean Communist] soldiers. Lately a member of the police station came to inspect about your personal history and we heard of your staying in a prisoner of war camp. I could not but be surprised hearing of your being alive because we believed that you would die somewhere. Fortunately it is very good for you.*
>
> *We hope that you are well. Don't worry about all your family. I am anxious for you to take care of yourself and do the best you can for our government.*
>
> *Yeong Pak Suk,*
your father

The letter proves undeliverable. A check turns up the fact that the addressee is a patient, possibly a hostage, in one of the holdout compounds. We don't even know whether he's alive or dead.

In midafternoon, with dull intensity, loudspeakers begin to blare a repeated theme into the besieged compounds. In effect: "Food is waiting for you—after you leave the compound and put your name on a roster. If you want to be repatriated—if you want to go back home— you must put your name on a roster which will be submitted to your leaders." The chattering of the loudspeakers goes on all day, all night, into the next morning. Even U.S. personnel are beginning to get worn down from the incessant babbling. But not one PW makes a move to comply. Instead, there is utter silence from within.

We sit in our huts in the heat, drinking Japanese beer and trying to drown out the loudspeakers with music on the short-wave radio: Beethoven and Brahms from Tokyo, Tschaikowsky from Moscow.

A scorching, sunny day—the hottest this year. Choking dust clouds make it even worse—not a wheel turns, nor a footstep made, without the dust churning up. We wonder how it's affecting the two compounds without direct access to water. We're up at sunrise, awakened by the incessant appeal of the loudspeakers and the counter-demonstrations of the PWs, who begin with the sun. In ONE and TWO the PWs are chanting over the chattering of the tireless loudspeakers what might be roughly translated as "We want food! We want medical care! And we want those damned loudspeakers turned off!"

Three PWs waving flags atop a Quonset hut in ONE are neatly picked off by three bullets fired from a rice paddy just outside the enclosure—identity of sharpshooter unknown. One is badly wounded, it seems; the others are less seriously hurt, probably more from their descent than from the shots. It's the very thing we've wanted to do ourselves for weeks, and there are grins from GIs and ROKs as they discuss the surprise assistance. But a big demonstration begins, as the PWs mass at the sally-port in ONE carrying their wounded on litters and demanding medical attention for them.

A surgeon arrives even before the procession reaches the gate, and shouts to the litter-bearers, "Carry them out."

"No, you come in and treat them inside," the PW spokesman insists, using English (although the surgeon had spoken in Korean).

160

Whether or not he has thoughts of Koje's compound 76 in mind, we do, and Capt. Bullock's answer is to the point—and this time in English: "Like hell I will!"

The Communists turn their backs on the medical team outside and carry their casualties back from the gate to the nearest hut. Now the insane screaming from ONE grows louder, even though the procession breaks up, and it rises above the din of the babbling loudspeakers, which—together with the hot sun—seem to be loosening their minds. Before long they return, hauling into view three flag-draped "bodies," purportedly the three PWs "killed" in the sniper's attack. It seems obvious to us that none bears any relation to the PWs just shot. Still, the three litters, covered with their makeshift flags, are placed "in state" near the main gate and a funeral service commences. The sun beats down; loudspeakers continue their din; PWs chant a funeral ritual, while those atop huts or near the inner barbed-wire fences scream oaths. Other compounds join in sympathetic demonstrations, and the pulsating noise seems to be exploding inside our own heads.

Suddenly the pounding loudspeakers cease, and— taken by surprise—the PWs fall silent; and the blessed quiet is palpable. Quickly we discover the cause—it seems to be a preliminary to the imminent arrival of International Red Cross representatives, en route from Koje. We grumble loudly at the news of their coming (since Communists do not allow inspection of their prison camps) and worry that IRC moral pressure may cancel our long-overdue pressure upon the PWs. Still,

161

they've had one positive effect—they've silenced the loudspeakers.

The IRC investigation team arrives and talks to PW leaders in tents set up for the purpose outside the compounds, with attendance of U.S. observers barred. Seeing the Americans shut out of the tents, and the deference paid to their spokesmen by the IRC representatives, is a moment of glory for the PWs; they cheer, wave their flags, and applaud loudly as the *honchos* enter the tent. But the PWs refuse to let the IRC view the victims of the shooting incident at ONE, or admit that any of the three wounded are alive and in need of medical care. Their own stubbornness loses them a few points, although the IRC team does not press the matter and goes through the motions of interviews with spokesmen of other compounds before departing. It is obvious from their parting talks with our officials that they're hardly in accord with our starve-out measures, or even with the principle of screening, for there is no clause in the Geneva Convention that permits the PWs any choice about repatriation.

Most officers and GIs are now standing around with little to do, since normal activities have been at a standstill. Only the crews detailed to the annex have regular employment, and they complain about the primitive facilities there, the uncomfortable commuting, and the increase of guerrilla interest in the establishment. At the main camp the gripes are different: the officers (especially M.D. variety) have less to do but the GI work load has increased, because enlisted men now must take care of all the housekeeping details—such as K.P.—formerly the responsibility of PW laborers. Besides, all sentry duty has been increased, and they must do double and triple the amount of guard duty they did before, each one serious now, rather than perfunctory.

The evening is so quiet that a movie is shown, with large attendance: *Since You Went Away*, a film of World War Two vintage, with Shirley Temple among others. Just the right kind of morale-boosting entertainment we need. I walk out, wander around the silent compounds to see what's doing—and then drift back in to see the movie through to the bitter end. The GI projectionist promises more current material soon: there's a film with Marilyn Monroe making the rounds of nearby units, and so far all that's been seen of her (and that's all of her) has been her calendar photo, which is just about everywhere in Korea. Our chief radiologist has had slides made from the most interesting of his astronomical collection of PW X rays, and whenever he shows them to curious visiting medical dignitaries he slips in a slide he's made from the calendar photo, with some such introductory remark as "Now this slide will give you an entirely different view of the chest."

A month has gone by now since the situation got out of hand. Quiet until sunup, the PWs are already busy with their too familiar demonstrations by the time I leave with my new assistant (in the admissions end of things) Lt. Cartier, for work preparatory to an IRC conference with the area general. The general wants detailed data on the holdout compounds even though such information is impossible to get. Apparently we have to defend our handling of the PW situation to the International Red Cross, although we have no authority to change it. Any change in the orders under which we are now operating would have to come from a higher command than the general's own. It's an impossible situation, for if we abandon coercion, as the Red Cross desires (in the interest of humane treatment of PWs), we must abandon the principle of voluntary repatriation (which is clearly a humane policy). Obviously we must risk a black eye in order not to repudiate our much publicized desires to guarantee free choice to each captive. Meanwhile the stalemate here and on Koje-do only intensifies the stalemate in the truce negotiations, and battle casualties and new PWs (some undoubtedly part of the Red courier system for keeping the pot boiling) keep coming in.

My harried look—yesterday a product of the loudspeakers—returns today because of the jangling of the telephone. Everybody with some semblance of authority in the truce talks or in the PW situation urgently wants the latest information and projections. Often the demand has an unrealistic time limit (all time limits are unrealistic, it seems) which has to be ignored. Sometimes a call temporarily elates us, as when we are asked to estimate how many flights in transport planes of the types generally used by the Far East Command would be needed to ferry to the thirty-eighth parallel all the badly disabled PWs who want to go home. We've been keeping a special box score of this, based on certain paragraphs in the Geneva Convention, and send some numbers in a hurry. Still, we expect to hear no more about it—the pattern of previous calls for such data.

Each time we have to call a number back we're now embarrassed by the notice on the cover of the phone book: "Your telephone offers no security against line tapping and listening in. Don't discuss classified matters." Many of our telephone conversations used to be carried on by PW clerks at our instructions, and almost certainly included potentially dangerous information. And many of these helpful—often zealous—clerks are now on Koje, having screened North! It was useful having them, because for every five minutes of talk there can be fifteen minutes of frustrating standing-by, while one goes from one temporary switchboard to another to get through to the one which had originally called for information. What a wonderful thing the dial system is!

The code names for unit telephones belie our naïve use of PW help before screening, for they've been made up ingeniously to trip up Orientals, who have difficulty pronouncing an *r* or an *l* distinctly: "Credit," "Rajah," "Ram," "Narcotic," "Gravy," "Bluebell," "Galveston,"

165

"Pennsylvania," "Rebate," "Radish," "Ragbag," (our own), "Rancho" (the British Command, of all things), "Ransack," "New Year," "Redhot," "Refund." . . . And up until recently, instead of this foiling the Communists, we've done everything but make them our switchboard operators, because they've been so eager and helpful.

Our PWs have even stopped using the compound phones to call us or each other. Whether they can do any listening in now, I don't know. Some noise comes from the compounds, but it appears to be petering out, especially from ONE. Few PWs seem to be leaving their huts and tents during daylight hours.

The live ones aren't bad enough: I'm having trouble with dead PWs again. Graves Registration calls, and a very irritated lieutenant—whose name I don't catch because of static on the telephone—complains that I've put him in hot water, for he's got to explain the fact that one of the dead on arrival (to us, from the line) Chinese Reds had the sum of 40,000 Won (South Korean) in his pockets. And we forwarded the body.

"Maybe it was planted on him," I suggest helpfully.

"Impossible!" he explodes. "And we can't put him in the ground with the loot, and if we report it we've got to explain it." (He can't get *too* mad at me because he's only a lieutenant also, and he may even be a second lieutenant.)

"Don't fret," I say. "Just send the money back to me with your name and address and I'll buy you a nice present in the Korean black market with it."

On hearing this suggestion, with the flouting of so many different Army regulations on so many different subjects implied, he almost goes into apoplexy on the other end of the line, and I don't understand a word of his answer, except what sounds like "Break it off"— which is Army lingo for good-bye on the crank-up (and crank-down) field phones. Or it could mean something else more personal here, perhaps. But I'm sure that's the last I'll hear on the matter. He must be an R.O.T.C. lieutenant.

He would have apoplexy if he knew of our unregistered graves. But I won't even let my corporal in charge of that operation, Digger Dempsey, tell me the locations, and I deliberately don't keep records or maps. Perhaps someday an archeologist several centuries from now—if mankind hasn't destroyed itself by then—will uncover a pit of human remains, a pile still recognizable as legs, or arms, and wonder what kind of people had such peculiar eating habits, or grisly rituals. They're the results of amputations at the hospital. We can't incinerate the fragments, for any shred of evidence of our burning flesh and bones might be inflated by the enemy into lurid tales of a Dachau or a Buchenwald. So Digger, in civilian life an undertaker's assistant from East St. Louis, loads up a truck with the materials to be disposed of in sacks, a couple of riflemen, and some husky PWs with picks and shovels. They go out, and up, to the most inaccessible place they can find, dig a deep hole, drop in their cargo, fill the hole, and replace the ground cover to blend with that rough territory. The next time around he tries another spot. Digger is the only G.I. I know of in all of Korea who likes his work.

Communist flags hang limply in the sultry air, and the protest posters and murals seem in need of retouching. Few PWs appear out of doors all day—none of the almost daily outdoors meetings and demonstrations we've been used to.

A little Chinese PW patient escapes somehow from ONE. All we know is that he was found on our side of the fence. He says that he doesn't want to go back, and that he is so hungry that when he stands up he becomes blind until he sits down for a little while. The Medical Officer of the Day has him fed and sent to the annex for further care. Obviously ONE is hurting first, as its food stockpile has no means of replenishment from fed compounds.

Meanwhile the only Communist prisoners still getting full, hospital-type medical and surgical treatment are the Communists among the ninety who were in the pre-op and post-op wards when the trouble began. In their own carefully tended and not so carefully guarded compound attached to the main hospital, they are the only human beings for miles around who sleep not only between clean sheets but on innerspring mattresses and steel hospital beds. The GIs who tend them don't have it nearly so good.

The wind picks up by evening, and the only motion, as far as can be seen in the twilight, is the fluttering of the sun-faded Communist flags.

A new medical officer has arrived to replace Capt. Lewis, who is scheduled to leave for home in a week. The Army must be getting efficient—not like what happened when Capt. Byers was due to go home last October. Then he sat here on his sack, chewing his nails and drinking, while his term of active duty ran out, and still no orders to go home, although he technically may have already become a civilian. The new man is another Navy doctor, on detached service.

We awakened Capt. Lesser, who seemed in the throes of a bad dream. He sat up with a start, and before we could ask him anything he blurted: "I was watching myself lead a beautiful girl—whom I intended to seduce—into a bedroom. Then I closed the door to keep me from seeing what I was going to do!"

"I had a lousy dream too," Capt. Lewis volunteered from down at the other end of the hut, without lifting his head from the sack, "—which is why I was up before everybody else. I was standing on the deck of the boat taking me back to the States. Just as we sighted land, the boat capsized."

The day doesn't seem to begin as if these are omens. It's cloudy and humid, and both the fed and unfed compounds seem quiet and listless. Few PWs seem to be walking around—none at all in ONE. Even the limp flags there are fewer. Shortly after dawn (I discover) three more PWs had escaped from ONE and asked to be screened South. They were fed and ferried by ambulance to the annex. Their story was that food shortage is weakening the resolve of the diehards, and that they were afraid all suspected anti-Communists would be done away with as a last gesture of defiance.

By 0930 it becomes obvious that ONE is preparing to give up quietly. At 1330, 175 able-bodied PWs line up by the sally-port and are permitted to straggle out, between a cordon of bayonet-wielding infantry. After the

PWs shuffle up the hill past TWO and THREE (both of which look quiet and deserted), other blue-scarved soldiers of the —th file into ONE with bayonets and billy clubs, and are followed by GI medical aid-men and doctors. Order is quickly restored, and guards are posted at the doors of each hut. Food and medicines are dispensed from waiting, trailing vehicles. One unreformed PW, sitting up in his cot, complains because no soup is being served. No one asks to be screened South, not even O Soo Sik.

All through the early morning hours the drone of a fleet of flying boxcar troop transports, first heard before daybreak, continues. An entire paratroop regiment is being ferried from Japan to the Korean mainland, to embark by ship immediately for Koje-do. A flush-out operation is in the works there, with the equivalent of a full division of additional troops on hand. In drawing these troops from other business, the PWs have made themselves militarily effective. Undoubtedly every propaganda advantage is being milked from the affair too.

I'm beginning to feel the effects of a bad cold, and ask the numerous doctors currently sitting on their hands what to do for it. First I'm told, "This is a PW hospital: we're only permitted by regulations to treat prisoners of war in this facility."

When I plead the seriousness of my case, the surgeons say, "We're cutting doctors, not talking doctors."

The practitioners of general medicine say, "Take a couple of aspirin tablets every few hours." They're a big help.

Infantrymen, removed from ONE during hours of darkness, move in again early in the morning and aid doctors and security officers in rounding up the ringleaders who escaped detection yesterday. All the known *honchos*—including "Blue-eyes," the surly chief spokesman for the compound—are herded together near the main gate. The able-bodied among them—few left, after yesterday—are put to work loading rubbish, debris of flags, banners and uniforms, and just plain garbage, into trucks. When it is clear that the manpower is insufficient, all remaining nonpatients in the compound are pressed into service, and when the job is done, all fifty-six are marched out and up the hill (temporarily) to vacant TEN.

During the afternoon a team of doctors, led by medical officers familiar with the cases in ONE, begins a housecleaning of patients, the criterion generally being that if a surgical patient is fit to join demonstrations, wave Red flags, and march in Communist parades, he's fit for discharge. Another 173 patients are discharged, with more earmarked for departure after a few days of further observation.

The total of discharges from ONE reaches about five hundred by late evening, and my men processing them, confused anyway by deliberate PW misidentifications, have reached the bewildered point. But they have the consolation of being able to notice that the arrogant leer which used to be the dominant expression seen in the

172

holdout compounds has been replaced, in ONE at least, by a sullen glare.

Screening goes unmentioned. When I bring up the subject that the very principle all this mess has been about has been overlooked in cleaning out ONE, I learn that screening of the nondischarged PWs will take place— after a fashion. The order is that patients remaining in ONE will not be asked about repatriation. If any who want to stay South volunteer such information, they'll be transferred to patient status in the annex.

Went to bed right after dinner to try to do something about my cold, and after a couple of hours began to feel better. But then the nagging hut phone prods me out of the sack to sit in on a meeting at the main hospital building. It lasts two and one-half hours, while I stare glassy-eyed at everyone. GHQ, it seems, is now jumpy about possible conditions in TWO and THREE, worried that the combination of coercion and possible starvation will cause this place to be described as another Dachau or Buchenwald.

I'm not impressed (in my semiconscious state it would be difficult to get through to me that convincingly anyway) and state with the deference necessary for one of my low rank that I see no reason to back down now since sufficient damage is already done for the Communist propaganda machine to get going, even if we backtrack. And if we don't stand by our principles and demands now, we'll have suffered another propaganda defeat anyway. None of this registers convincingly, so I point out that it would be a strained parallel to equate our long-suffering patience and record of medical care

173

with Nazi tactics, in spite of the PW sign that apparently impressed the IRC officials.

Nevertheless, I'm told that we must explain (or justify) to headquarters all the deaths of PWs reported since we began our withholding of rations. The death rate is normal, I explain—even below normal, as far as known deaths are concerned. For we're actually operating half a hospital, which makes the known evidence no cause for alarm. Of course what kind of situation we'll discover in the besieged wards we don't know, for we have no check yet on concealed murders or deaths. But in these cases neither the concealment nor the deaths are our doing anyway.

What about reported deaths from starvation or malnutrition? I realize that this is the key point and has been ever since the Chinese PW escaped from ONE, even though we have since found no serious case of malnutrition in ONE. "Negative," is all that can be said, and I say it. Still, I'm told to be prepared to explain to higher command if asked; and the definite impression is left with us that GHQ would rather see us flush out the prisoners forcibly now than let us withhold food any longer. We'd be just as glad to get the agony over with.

The cloudy, humid weather of the last few days has turned into an all-day drizzle, and I try to keep under a roof as much as possible. Early in the morning the expected phone call comes through, asking for a rush report on the deaths so far in the closed compounds since the screening began. This turns out to be no trouble at all to compile: ONE, TWO, and THREE in the last five weeks have each dragged only one body to the gate for disposal. (It almost seems as if they've thrived more on curtailed medical care than they might have if they had been exposed to the full medical works!) We're asked about the three bodies for which the PWs in ONE had held a funeral ceremony on the day the IRC officials came. The answer is the same: we don't know anything about them. Never found any inside.

A full alert is ordered on again. In the morning, at ration-delivery time, THREE and TWO are informed that they'll be fed if the *honchos* and all nonpatients line up at the sally-port gate for transfer to TEN. The loudspeakers get no response. No sound or activity in either compound; no PW in sight all day. The gloomy drizzle continues to fall, and toward evening, in the rain, a few PW sentinels are seen. The popular theory is that all PWs remain in their huts by orders of the chief *honchos,* so that we can't see that they are disposing of food from their neighboring compounds—which they probably get surreptitiously at night. We keep guessing as to their actual condition.

175

A night meeting is called. We're to move into THREE at dawn tomorrow. If the Communists fail to respond to appeals to emerge peacefully, the infantry will flush them out—if possible, without firing a shot. The final report on ONE is that of all the PWs removed from the compound, only thirteen have asked to stay South—an indication of how many fanatical Communists there were in ONE. Most of that compound's patient population cannot be discharged, because their surgical problems are too severe for outpatient treatment, but the enclosure is more like a hospital ward again. Still present are the two best-known patients, known to the doctors as "Half-face" and "No-face"—names that sound more like Dick Tracy than reality. But it indicates the extent of their wounds.

Capt. Lewis queried No-face about why he decided to screen North, since he probably could get better medical care here. "But I won't be here all my life, because you won't be. What good will I be to the Koreans, or even to the Nationalists [on Formosa]," he said, "without eyes and without a nose? But back home in China I'll be a hero, even if I'm not good to look at. And my brother has a basket factory. I won't be good for very much, but probably I can help make baskets and feel useful. It has nothing to do with politics."

The drizzle lessens by evening, and a blanket of fog settles over the camp, but preparations go ahead for a possible forced entry into THREE.

There is no sun at dawn: it is a gray, damp day, with a steady, light rain falling. No sound has come from either of the holdout compounds all night. At 0630 a sound truck pauses by the main gate at THREE to warn all PWs inside to mass at the gate for orderly movement to TEN. The order refers to separation of patients from nonpatients, and no mention is made of screening or repatriation. Not a sound comes from the compound, and the order is repeated, with the added warning that if peaceful movement is not possible, all PWs will be forcibly escorted to the new compound. Still, no life is visible in the compound, each ward so quiet that the drip of rain from hut roofs is audible.

Finally troops of the —th are ordered to mass on all sides of the compound, and they fan out, a large force remaining at the main gate. As soon as the PWs notice this deployment, the lone North Korean flag high above the compound, drooping damply in the mist, is hauled down by two agile Communists who clamber up the slippery roof of the hut (where a printed message warning us away is oozing off in the rain). They and the flag disappear inside the hut, leading us to wonder whether they are going to surrender peacefully or whether the flag has been taken down to prevent its capture.

We wait, but there is no further sign of life within, and it is obvious that the PWs do not intend peaceful compliance. The main gate to THREE is gingerly opened, and a company of infantry moves cautiously into the compound. From the compound's mess hall, near the gate, Communists rush out to the attack, and the GIs momentarily retreat under a flurry of rocks and homemade spears and javelins. A lone tank bursts through the barbed wire near the gate, smashes across the blockade of debris and into the PW mess hall, just far enough to leave a gaping rent in the wall, over which the roof begins to buckle. Simultaneously the returning infantrymen, as the tank backs out slightly, heave tear-gas bombs into the opening, evicting the remaining occupants. From the other side of the compound, PWs in the amputee ward—there are seven hundred of them—rush out of their huts with crude spears and barbed-wire flails, Molotov-cocktail bombs and rocks. Concussion grenades are tossed in their path and explode with a roar—more sound and shock than fury, but fury enough if one explodes too close. The amputees are forced back into their ward, and the infantrymen press their advantage, moving ahead with bayonets fixed.

Another infantry company forces its way into the compound from the opposite end, near its junction with SIX, its aim to clear all the huts in the north and east sectors, and to force all PWs to the cleared recreation area in the southwest corner of the compound. The Communists refuse to budge until tear gas is used: the fumes are blinding, but the PWs come out fighting before beating a retreat. When they fall back, infantrymen with gas masks pour into the compound and press forward; and as the PWs evacuate each gas-filled hut, the battalion colonel calls on the personnel stationed on the inner perimeter of the compound to use a favorite PW device—rock heaving—to drive the Communists away from the gate to SIX and toward the open recreation area. From the plateau a hail of rocks follows, but some PWs escape into the deathlike quiet of SIX anyway, and disappear into nearby huts.

Quickly the escape route into SIX is plugged by warning gunfire from tanks on the plateau. Fifty-caliber tracer bullets spray above the Communists' heads, then ricochet crazily into the mist over the compound as red and yellow streaks. Most PWs react by retreating to the recreation clearing, where shouted instructions to them are to squat there with hands in back of their heads. Stubborn holdouts are routed out of crevices and dugouts and corners of wrecked huts with the sharp roar of concussion grenades and the prodding of rump-piercing bayonets.

In the fence-enclosed fourth ward, the seven hundred amputees still resist fanatically. They have aluminum litter poles, honed to razor sharpness at one end, and also a supply of wooden tent poles whittled to a point. As infantrymen close in, they heave a fusillade of crude grenades made of casting plaster studded with fragments of barbed wire and nails. Exploding tear-gas canisters fill the ward with pungent white smoke; and then, cutting their way into the ward with wire shears, GIs stream through the openings in the barbed wire, ignoring the trash-blockaded gates.

The yelling amputees, with accompanying able-bodied PW aid-men, stumble back into the mist, throwing their weapons as—now disorganized—they retire. A one-legged PW, moving rapidly and jerkily with the aid of a crutch, is stopped in midmotion of throwing a spear by an over-thrown concussion grenade. It hits directly in front of him, and his remaining leg is shattered. The crutch lands a dozen yards away, apparently undamaged. A bilateral amputee crawls out of his gas-filled hut on his stumps, leans against the side of his hut for support, and aims a sharpened litter pole at a passing GI, who sees him just in time. Clobbered over the head with a rifle butt, the PW tumbles into a muddy drainage ditch, the spear bouncing in after him. GI medics following behind pull him out, but leave the spear stuck crazily in the ditch bank.

A groping infantryman, just inside the ward, halts be-latedly to tug on his gas mask, his eyes already watering. As he settles it into place, a barbed-wire-and-plaster missile hits him directly on the mask, knocking him down on his back. Getting up slowly in the mist and drizzle, he rises dazedly only to his knees and goes no farther.

Another concussion grenade lands on the roof of a hut and explodes, blowing a huge opening, through which the mist of tear gas rises. The PWs, who had with-stood the fumes inside, find the roar and shock waves of the grenade too much to take, and straggle out through a gap a simultaneous explosion had made in one of the walls. Actually the hut is in better shape now because of the ventilation. But one Communist amputee lies dead in a pool of blood near the gap in the wall. For some reason I jot down the location as hut #3.

Restoration of order comes rapidly now. The Commu-nists are forced to huddle in the open part of the com-pound, which is relatively free from tear gas. Meanwhile the medical screening teams have moved in directly behind the infantrymen. The serious new casualties are pulled out and evacuated to the main hospital for emergency care and surgery (sixty operations performed by midnight). The screening teams file methodically through the eye-stabbing atmosphere of the huts to extricate the bedridden and the groping victims of tear-gas exposure. Minor cases—patients fit for discharge—and nonpatients are weeded out, lined up, and marched up the hill to TEN for screening (and, very likely, Koje). They stubbornly begin singing the North Korean Red Army song, but only manage the first few bars. The march is halted, and several rifle butts thud. The march then proceeds silently.

Rain continues to fall lightly, and the moisture-laden atmosphere keeps the pungent tear gas clinging to the ground. In the gloom medical officers, wearing gas masks rather than surgical masks, are examining patients who apparently are not ambulatory. In the amputee ward their criteria for discharge of patients not newly wounded is simple: if they have one leg, they go; if they have none, they remain. Merely a matter of counting. Those with superficial new wounds—mostly bruised heads or punctured buttocks—are patched and trucked up the hill to TEN, and the ward gradually empties.

Only seventeen of the evacuated PWs ask to stay South —all that are left of the anti-Communists in the tightly Red-controlled compound. The Communist fanaticism persists even through the screening process—many give false names or none at all, hoping to keep us from ever knowing what actually went on in THREE. One Communist PW, I discover, has a fistful of PW identity cards, which are seized before he has a chance to dispose of them. Wondering whether they might be evidence of murdered and hidden hostages, I ask him where he got them. Unreconstructed, he tells me—with a bizarre sense of humor—that he was using them to learn how to read English.

Inspection proves that much food is still around. The compound, though, is a shambles. Some huts are skeletons; practically every hut has suffered damage sufficient to make it uninhabitable. Seventy-one PWs, bedridden among the debris and fumes (but not newly injured), are evacuated on litters to the few huts still with four walls and a roof. By twilight the job is done, and a huge pyre lights the sky, as Communist flags, signs, and wreckage are sent up in flames. They crackle with their dampness; a steady drizzle still falls.

On the way back to the hut I pass the mess hall and realize that I don't remember whether I've had anything to eat today. The cook is in a jolly mood and supplies some fried Spam and scrambled (powdered) eggs and a can of condensed milk. "I don't have any more coffee ready, sir," he grins. "Just add some water to that and pretend it's milk." In twos and threes, more latecomers drift in to be fed, and before long the aroma of coffee pervades, mixing strangely with the odor of tear gas renewing itself in the atmosphere with each new arrival from duty at THREE.

Back at the hut Lt. Jenks, resting in the sack after a full day's work as cutting doctor again, tells me that business was so good that the operating rooms briefly

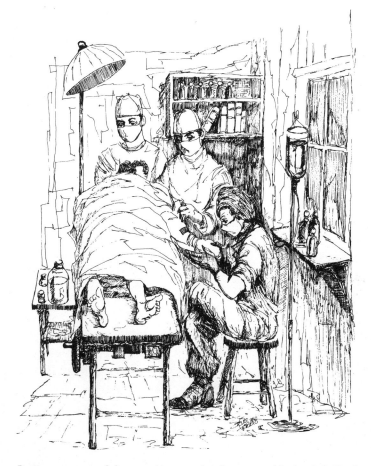

Business was so good the operating rooms briefly ran out of fresh, whole blood.

ran out of fresh, whole blood at one crucial point. When nothing else would do for injection into the veins of a PW casualty who showed critical post-operative weakening, Navy surgeon Bob McDowell tapped his own veins to transfuse the patient.

"Did it work, Herb?"

"No, he expired soon after we got him off the table."

It is nearly midnight when I pull off my wet clothes. They reek so of tear gas that they still make my eyes smart. Nor does the odor wash off easily. I tug the blankets over me, and a wave of tear gas floats up. The thought occurs to me that this may have been the first time a hospital's patients were discharged by an infantry battalion.

The fog blanketing the enclosure lifts at sunrise. By 0600, infantrymen are massed around the uneven rectangle enclosing TWO (which takes up three of the corners), SEVEN (the large lower corner to our right), and the evacuated Admissions and Dispositions area (a small square front and center, between TWO and SEVEN). Unlike yesterday, all personnel wear gas masks, giving the setting an other-worldly appearance. A sound truck blares into TWO a variation of the familiar ultimatum: all PW laborers and ward attendants are to mass at the sally-port gate for transportation to another compound; all ambulatory patients are then to mass at the same gate for medical screening. Again, nothing is said about political screening or repatriation. The operation is not expected to affect the neuropsychiatric ward—the heavily fenced enclosure taking up the front and left corner in TWO. It is not expected that it will involve SEVEN either, although we assume that SEVEN has continued to keep TWO supplied with rations.

As a token gesture (for PWs have gone in and out at will), M.P.s enter the Admissions and Dispositions area and open the gate into TWO. The encouragement goes unheeded, for at first no one is visible or audible in either TWO or SEVEN. The ten minutes allotted for the beginning of compliance expires, and still there is no sign of movement within the compound. On prearranged order, troops with fixed bayonets and gas masks move into the sally-port inside the main gate and filter to the left and to the right through openings in the fence made by wire shears. Meanwhile another company of infantrymen cuts through the barbed wire and proceeds through TWO from the northwest corner just above SEVEN. PW monitors in SEVEN make their appearance and look on silently and curiously. All is quiet: not a Communist stirring. Tear gas billows out of huts in the rear of the compound, but no PWs emerge.

Troops hack at the closed doors of the huts with the butts of their rifles and rip out the canvas and plywood walls with slashes of their bayonets. Unbelievingly they turn from hut to hut amid silent puffs of tear gas and then cut their way warily into the neuropsychiatric enclosure. Not a PW is found anywhere in the compound —of a total of well over a thousand supposed to have been there. The reason for the lack of activity in the compound now becomes obvious: since the PWs could not have evaded our heavily augmented perimeter guard, they, aided in recent nights by a protective blanket of fog, must have been slipping into SEVEN through shallow tunnels under the barbed wire between the compounds. The tiny compound, we realize, must now be jammed with nearly two thousand prisoners—but the only ones in sight are the Communists' own sentries, now patrolling impassively beside each silent hut and tent. We look at each other in bewilderment. How they all could possibly have been evacuated into SEVEN without our knowledge or suspicion is a mystery, yet no other conjecture is possible. Though TWO contained hundreds of able-bodied (or at least ambulant) fanatics, it

187

also housed—we shake our heads incredulously—patients seriously ill with far-advanced tuberculosis, and both board-rigid catatonic schizophrenics and wildly mad strait-jacket cases. Now it is ghostly vacant.

The —th's commanding officer strides to the sound truck, picks up the microphone, and orders SEVEN cleared: all PWs are directed to line up five abreast in front of the gate—immediately—or we will go in and get them. An interpreter repeats the message first in Korean and then in Chinese, and before the Chinese version has ended, PWs begin emerging from the huts and lining up. But there is obviously not half the number we anticipate in the column. Inspired by their gain in "face" resulting from the fanatically futile maneuver, they begin to chant Communist songs and raise fists in Red salute—a last, stubborn gesture of defiance. Ordered to be silent, they refuse. Suddenly tear-gas grenades are lobbed in, and they scatter through the piercing white smoke in disorder. Another fusillade of grenades follows, and those PWs hiding in the huts scramble out, eyes streaming, in groping confusion. The compound now looks like an anthill which has been overturned.

The surliness and arrogance disappears. They are led out one hundred at a time to be screened medically. The able-bodied are marched to TEN, now empty again as yesterday's occupants are already en route to Koje. Barely more than a fifth are retained as patients, but the screening is vindictively hasty, and some of the marchers are unable to negotiate the hill and have to be returned. A head count shows forty-three PWs "missing" from two compounds, some of whom were undoubtedly earlier escapees. Our casualties of the operation: none. Communist: two with bayonet punctures of the buttocks. They are patched and sent up the hill.

The report on the day's political screening comes in surprisingly rapidly this time. Seventy-three (including one North Korean captain and one Chinese captain) ask to stay South. The screening problem was complicated by the fact that those who belonged in SEVEN had already screened North but were mixed up with the unscreened PWs from TWO, and some PWs from both compounds refused to identify themselves—even whether or not they were patients. All such have to be screened North and assumed not to be patients, unless a fingerprint check proves otherwise someday.

We look out upon another quarter of a square mile of wreckage—all that is left of TWO and SEVEN. In THREE, huge piles of debris are still being burned, a result of our having to fight for each hut.

Another kind of fight is in prospect now: the struggle to find out where we are. On paper, despite our efforts to keep up with the fantastic confusion, we still have the impossible task of effecting administratively the discharge of thousands of patients who not only are already miles away from here, but many of whom furnished different names on leaving from those they gave on arriving. Many identities will undoubtedly remain in permanent limbo, for even many of those wanting to stay South don't want to identify themselves for fear of family reprisals at home, preferring, rather, to be thought as having been killed in action or having died in prison camp. It's a Kafka kind of situation: I feel like the man condemned to put together a mammoth jigsaw puzzle; and though he has many more pieces that he can possibly fit into the puzzle, he doesn't have all the right ones to fit the empty spaces. And there are thousands of pieces, all in a strange language.

Late at night I officially transmit a rush request through channels to get a month's delay in submission of the end-of-the-month records and reports, giving such reasons as the wholesale discharges, *effected after forced segregation of patients within hospital compounds, ward records suffering destruction, identification of many prisoner of war patients in doubt, and admininstrative facilities severely taxed.* . . .

At four in the morning the hut phone rings: a guerrilla raid is reported in progress at an engineer battalion post between here and the hospital annex. A follow-up report in twenty minutes is that the Communists have captured two machine guns, ammunition, and small arms in a fairly large-scale attack for this area. Two GIs wounded; two ROKs wounded. And five GIs—dead on arrival—are brought here in an annex ambulance, escorted by an armed jeep. Several of the dead are barefoot, their feet scratched and bloody. While I wonder whether the guerrillas robbed the GIs of their boots—valuable commodities in Korea—one of the men from the accompanying jeep notes my questioning glance. "We figure they must have been surprised out of their sleep and hadn't a chance. . . ." His voice trails off.

In the wan light of early dawn we unload the DOAs, and I note dangling from a limp wrist an identification

190

bracelet with a familiar surname: although the GI is not (as far as I know) related to me, his surname is one common in my family.

Walking back to the huts with the Medical Officer of the Day, we look for other things to talk about, trying to evade the subject of the five GIs, who never had a chance; but eventually we turn to the raid. If its purpose was possible guerrilla aid to the holdout Communist prisoners, I suggest, it was about twenty hours too late. There will be no further such opportunity on the mainland of Korea.

My request for authority to delay submission of the end-of-the-month medical reports and statistics required by regulations comes back in two teletyped words: "not granted." We'll appeal in writing, but it's the only really funny thing that's happened in the last five weeks. Renewed in spirit, we bend to our tasks.

Afterword

Although we learned a lot from our experience, we could apply very little of it in the intervening months when the war was cooling down and truce negotiations were dragging on. After separating hard-core Communists from the other PWs, we automatically became less security-conscious regarding the "non-Communist" PWs. Despite their isolation, enemy infiltrators undoubtedly had penetrated that group to seed trouble. Meanwhile the hard-core enemy became even more inflexible. Worst of all, our dependence on ROK soldiers for much of the guard duty meant that anything could still happen. This poorly paid, badly treated force suffered from a corruption of their officer corps which reached into the highest levels. We could do nothing about it, even after such repeated intelligence complaints as one we received on July 14, 1952:

> *We have definite evidence that there is a lack of security . . . and that the PWs have contact with prostitutes and black marketeers through the connivance of a ROKA Capt and M/Sgt who live in a thatched-roof hut near the north fence . . . ROK guards cut the fence to let out PWs between 0100 and 0200 to meet prostitutes in this house, where they drink and have sexual intercourse. A short time costs 30,000 Won.* The PWs exchange drugs, clothing and blankets for Won. The PWs also have access there to Korean newspapers. Appropriate steps should be taken to insure better security.*

---

* $3 U.S. at black market exchange rates then; $5 at legal rates.

There were no appropriate steps. Sometimes the thatched-roof hut or its equivalent would be torn down and the ROK officer replaced. Sometimes he was protected. In any case, his replacement would be just as likely to go into business for himself.

In the aftermath of the war in the wards and the decrease in the size of the hospital, some personnel were transferred and at least one disappeared — Evelyn Smith. Just disappeared. AWOL. She was later discovered back in the States, as a patient in an army hospital. She had gone off with a paratroop officer, a case of whiskey and promises that she would be taught to jump. I think she entertained ideas of someday bailing out over China. On the third jump she landed wrong and returned home encased in plaster. I am sure the affair was handled quietly and her days in the army terminated. In any case, we missed her.

The pencilled entries in my notebooks and note-pad sheets are beginning to fade badly now, but some of the later entries suggest the way things went in the aftermath of the hospital siege.

June 4

Quadruple amputee in FOUR commits suicide by hanging himself. Quite a trick. (None of our information indicated that he had any ideological enemies. It was quite possible that he did want to end his life and received some help. But no one talked.)

196

June 22

Borrowed an ambulance — they're mostly unused right now — and went to the beach with a doctor and two nurses. Long, dusty ride but worth it. About 150 yards of sandy beach labelled "For U.S. Forces Only." Nothing in sight but a few fishing sampans: almost as if there were no war. Returned to find a drowning in the *benjo* in SIX.* Was it murder or accident? We don't know. Immediately thought of the song, "I didn't slip; I wasn't pushed; I fell." Then felt guilty about it. Autopsy being done on the victim.

July 26

Borrowed an ambulance and three of us managed about ninety minutes at the beach. The inlet fjord-like. No waves, just a strong undertow in the very buoyant, salty water. Singularly quiet; no roar of breakers or cries of gulls; no inane chatter of holiday bathers and no board-walk. Sampans and a lumbering freighter in the distance.

August 16

Begin shipping NK Communist patients to Koje, where hospital has been expanded. Will transfer 835 tomorrow

* See foreword for the details.

morning and over the next four days. Then we will send 600 Chinese to another island, Cheju. It suggests a long war — that we'll be holding them a long time.

August 19

Typhoon halts PW exodus, except for a few attempted escapes under cover of storm. Rare clean smell in the air afterwards.

August 23

Storm continues; nothing moving in the mud, wind and rain except the contents of my hut, which is flooded.

October 1

Planeload of wounded Chinese PWs arrives. Several hold their hands over their testicles as they're carried in, for Red propaganda is that we castrate all we capture.

October 24

Head north to check on why live Chinese PWs are now seldom in the pipeline but why there is an increased need for Chinese death certificates. Take a load of UN Form

#13 (death certificate, Chinese) with me on a flying box-car to Chunchon, just below the 38th parallel, and to Seoul.

November 6

Back at work but weak after a bout of bacillary dysentery, and still on chloromycetin. Difficult task, running to out-house when wobbly, in unlaced combat boots, and in mud and driving rain. No one very excited about out-come of presidential election, assuming either candidate would have to end the war with some compromise.

February 3

Pay last business call on Koje, going via AK-31, a cargo and passenger shuttle boat. Takes from dawn to 1100. New CO on the island has erected ten-foot-high white crosses at each location where something traumatic oc-curred: "8 PWs FOUND DEAD IN THIS DITCH IN COMPOUND #76, 10 JUNE 1952," or "2 PWs FOUND DEAD IN THIS WELL, 11 JUNE 1952." Since they're in English they must be to impress future tourists, if there will be any.

The two down-valley annexes for TB patients only are each now bigger than the main Koje hospital. At Annex 1, I encounter an old sparring partner, the PW former Pyongyang schoolmaster who was the chief visible *honcho* in SIX during the screening. He grins and bows, as usual, and tells me in faultless English that he's very happy. I ask him if he's still a *honcho*, and he protests that he never was — which means he still is.

Everyone expects the fighting to end soon. Few PWs taken now.

Totting up the score before leaving, I discovered that the mainland hospital had admitted and treated almost 90,000 patients. All but 477 of them were allegedly PWs when admitted. In addition, the staff treated over a quarter of a million outpatients and performed nearly thirteen thousand surgical operations. I never counted up the number of recorded dead-on-arrival. It had been quite a place.

On the last day of February, 1953, almost a year after the war in the wards had ended, I left for home and separation from service. By then the situation in Korea had radically changed, but the war was not yet over. All screened-South Koreans who claimed to have originally been civilians living south of the thirty-eighth parallel had not only been classified (over Red protests) as civilian internees, but segregated in separate mainland camps. Later (over American protests), wily old Syngman Rhee let his ROK troops throw open the gates and send the 22,000 "civilians" into dubious freedom. Meanwhile, the fighting on the line was spotty yet fierce. Casualties kept trickling back, although not in the flood of the first year of war. The PW patient population continued to shrink even though some of the PWs discharged at bayonet point eventually returned from exile on Koje-do for rehospitalization.

Koje, meanwhile, as the note about the white crosses indicates, had undergone a vast change. After a segregation procedure that followed the mutinies, only screened-North prisoners remained on the island. Compound 76, which had seized Dodd, was pacified on June 10, 1952, after fierce Communist resistance with the usual improvised weapons. Compound 77 then submitted without a battle, and, one after another, the remaining holdout compounds were broken up and anti-Communist prisoners removed. By the time of my February 1952 visit, Koje was relatively quiet.

Repatriation for PWs still seemed far away as I embarked for home. Many false alarms about an armistice, even about an exchange of sick and wounded prisoners, had ended each time in futile, frustrating work on preliminaries, which, whenever negotiations failed, had to be revised according to the current situation. The truce talks then seemed likely to outdistance in length and number of sessions even Scheherezade's famous series, and they often had the same quality of fantasy.

While I was re-crossing the Pacific, news of Stalin's death foreshadowed a spring thaw. On April 11, shortly after I returned to civilian life, "Operation Little Switch" —the exchange of sick and wounded PWs—was agreed upon. Finally on July 27, 1953, came the armistice. "Operation Big Switch" — the mass exchanges of prisoners — lasted into early autumn. Twenty-two thousand screened-South Chinese and Korean PWs, given under the truce agreement a further opportunity to choose to return, again declined. But in the United States, behind the Iron Curtain and in the uncommitted nations around the

201

world, the event was overshadowed by the fact that twenty-one American PWs decided to stay in Communist China and North Korea.

American newspapers and magazines, I discovered later, had reported the final stages of our small war in the sprawling PW hospital in a few laconic sentences, mentioning only that patients who had resisted transfer from one ward to another had rioted, leaving two dead and some dozens injured. The incident (for, except to us, that's all the "war" really amounted to) was overwhelmed by other reports about PWs from Koje, and by other news in general. Even the Communist propaganda mill (having found so much other rewarding material in the Koje kidnapping and in the fiction about germ warfare in Korea) failed to manufacture the predictable quota of half-truth from the event. A miniscule confrontation between Communist and Western minds, the eerie war in the wards had faded from history without ever achieving even the ephemeral dignity of becoming "news."